A SINGLE MOTHE.. ... ... THE DATING GAME

Tips on how to manoeuvre

the dating minefield

By

MARGARET THORLI

Copyright © 2022

"I'll love me, however, whenever, wherever; because there's only ONE of ME"

WE ACCEPT
THE LOVE
WE THINK
WE DESERVE.

H&R
TRAINING
PROFESSIONALS

TABLE OF CONTENTS

"I know I have the capacity to be remarkable, don't believe me–just watch this space!"

DISCLAIMER

The information contained in this book is for general information purposes only. The information is provided by Margaret Thorli and while we endeavour to keep the information up to date and correct, we make no representations or warranties of any kind, express or implied, about the completeness, accuracy, reliability, suitability or availability with respect to this publication or the information, products, services, or related graphics contained in this publication for any purpose. Any reliance you place on such information is therefore strictly at your own risk.

In no event will we be liable for any loss or damage including without limitation, indirect or consequential loss or damage, or any loss or damage whatsoever arising from loss of data or profits arising out of, or in connection with, the use of this publication.

Through this publication you are able to link to other resources and contacts which are not under the control of Margaret Thorli. We have no control over the nature, content and availability of those responsible for their management, operation or function. The inclusion of any links does not necessarily imply a recommendation or endorse the views expressed within them.At the time of writing, every effort was made to keep the information in this publication current. However, Margaret Thorli takes no responsibility for, and will not be liable for, information being out of date or unavailable due to technical or any other issue beyond our control.

DEDICATED

This book is firstly dedicated to God, my best friend who brought me out alive through the many storms of life and dating.

"I must be the change I want to see in the world"

ACKNOWLEDGEMENTS

I would like to thank everyone who supported me in bringing this
book to life especially my beautiful sons
-love you both loads.

"Our life is an endless journey; it's like a broad highway
extending infinitely into the distance. All's not lost and this is just
the beginning for me"

INTRODUCTION

A Single Mother and the Dating Game: Tips on how to Manoeuvre the Dating Minefield provides personal experiences that many single mothers may identify with; from the emotional turmoil of being single and a mother, caring for young children, to trying to manage a household while still holding down a job or starting a business, from overseeing finances to being flexible when going on dates; all of which make for a difficult process. Single Mother and the Dating Game: Tips on how to Manoeuvre the Dating Minefield attempts to lift the veil on this issue by providing candid examples, moving stories and tangible tips. I hope you find this book useful and I encourage you to look out for the upcoming workshops, where you will be empowered by learning from the practical exercises and guidance on offer.

Please enjoy my book, A Single Mother and the Dating Game: Tips on how to Manoeuvre the dating minefield.

Margaret Thorli

THIS IS ME, NOW

"I need to take the first step into my future by believing in myself"

I Am Not Afraid

I am not afraid of not getting a text generally;

But I am afraid of sitting here staring at my phone, in my hand waiting for it to ring,

Or a WhatsApp to come,

Or worrying I may be dumped by text. I am not afraid of going on a date,

I am afraid of wasting my precious time on the wrong man. Now, my time is very precious,

The valuable things I possess I cannot afford to waste on a dead-end date that will bring me nothing but heartache.

I would rather spend my time with people of substance that I like having around me, than being with a man who might bring nothing but   baggage.

I am not afraid of being myself.

I am afraid of being with someone,

Who may make me feel like I cannot be.

I do not have it in me to be anything other than myself, completely and wholly.

 I am not afraid of being without a plus one,

I am afraid that the one will turn out to be Mr. Embarrassment and a misfit.

I am getting used to going to parties without a plus one; even though there were times I wished to have someone to go with me, holding hands whispering sweet nothings in my ear.

I am afraid the next one might not be the one. But not afraid of being cold and alone in bed.

I am afraid of being vulnerable, used, rejected and broken hearted,

Feeling worthless, brutally dumped, and emotionally drained.

I am not afraid of being alone.

I'm afraid of being with someone who would make me feel empty, unhappy, and unappreciated.

Or in a relationship that would make me feel lonelier than ever I had when I was single.

"Step into the unknown and enjoy"

THE BIG FEAR

With both of my sons having grown up, the eldest leaving home and the youngest still living with me, turning eighteen, I no longer had the responsibility of being at home at any particular time to ensure he was okay. As time went on, he was going out more and more, having the freedom to do whatever he wanted; like coming home late.

But the reality was, I feared being alone, hopeless, rejected and lost since my life no longer revolved around him. Though I was fearful of loneliness, I did not allow myself to enter into any relationship that would bring nothing but unhappiness, tears, abuse or lack of fulfilment. Although I knew the day would come when my youngest will no longer be around, I still was not prepared for it.

How could I be ready for the time when my last child came of age?

I was too afraid of waking up to a total stranger thinking 'why was he in my bed?' So, instead of sharing my bed with a stranger who may bring unhappiness, I might as well keep that sacred and lonely space until I found the right person who would love and accept me for who I am. Since I no longer had the energy, time or patience for the awkward morning goodbyes.

I had refused to go on dates because I did not want to bring too many men into my home and was afraid of dating one who may have seemed right, at the time, but later turned out to be as wrong as ever.

When I was younger, I did not care if I dated for short or long periods, always ensuring I enjoyed myself for the duration. I even made sure my own baggage, especially around vulnerability or worry, did not find its way into the date.

It was all about control and if that failed, I would tell myself there were more fish in the sea. But I no longer think that way. Now, I no longer seek a partner who I know has the potential to break my heart, or would like to have a one night stand or booty call. I have outgrown that type of dating and no longer waste precious time on a man who does not bring value into my life and for sure, I no longer sit around waiting, wondering if a text or call was coming my way.

I do admit it was not me being on my own that scared me; it was the process of finding someone who I eventually considered to be unworthy. Unworthy of me or my time, energy and love. Here in my golden age (so to speak) and being out of the dating game for a while, I do not wish to kiss too many frogs in the hope they turned into my Prince

 Charming; nor having the need to go fishing a few times before I found that dream man.

Future Events Appearing Real is never real. Never be afraid to venture in anything you want and wish to do.

"Never let another say you're not worthy, good or great enough; the Creator ordained that you should be here…nobody and no one else but you – YOU are more than worthy!"

THE BEGINNING OF MY JOURNEY

"It's not how I started,

What's important is how I finish"

YOUNG, SINGLE AND OH, SO FREE!

When I was young, single and dating, the world was my oyster! I was free and fearless, dating anybody I wanted and running my businesses. I had my own money and very successful in my own right and when it came to dating, I was happy! Full of confidence, taking time to explore the various relationships that were open to me before I decided if I wanted to settle down.

I always wanted to fall in love but organically and at my own pace and with the right person. There were things I liked when I was single and dating; like the opportunity to explore those entire 'ifs'. Say for instance, meeting a random person at some party or an acquaintance I may have had a crush on for some time, I loved exploring if things could work out between us without worrying what if it did not and If not, I was able to walk away knowing my confidence was not dented. Being single and pursuing the 'what-ifs' and where they may lead was fun and exciting.

In those days, being young and single with no children was nice, staying out as long as I wanted or getting up late or as early as I wanted. I was free and if I got a call inviting me somewhere, I would be up, dressed and ready to go. There were so many times I had long quiet weekends, away from home, visiting interesting places on my own or reading a book, only getting up to make a cup of tea or use the bathroom before returning to bed - those were the days!

Now those days will never return; the long walks, traveling, nights out with mates and no worries about children other than myself. Those were the days!

When I Was Single – the reason

Whether a young or an older single parent, this book was written for you to read. For you to know you're not alone, going through the issue of dating and to help you move on with your life while enjoying the dating game. Being out of the dating game for a long time left me, feeling scared and it was difficult for me to leave my comfort zone behind. The difficulties I faced during the first few months when looking to date, difficulties like making time to meet, visiting new places, bringing him to my home to my children, friends and family; these all had their challenges. Things such as him meeting my children, for instance, were a huge concern for me - would they like him? Were they going to give him a hard time? Would he fit in with my circle of friends?

Questions swam in my head, some of which I was unable to answer and often kept telling myself I would cross that bridge whenever I got to it.

Miss Too Busy

Being self-employed, my time is essential and at one time, a person I was dating misunderstood that. He would call me during the hours of 10am to 1pm when I would be in the middle of teaching or in a 1-2-1 business coaching session. So, I was unable to pick

up his calls or talk to him. In the end, he would call me
'"Miss Too Busy" which annoyed me. I repeatedly told
him not to call me that but it fell on deaf ears and in
the end, he had to go. We were both   on different
wavelengths.

Scared Of the Unknown

One day while watching the news about a woman
who met a man on an online dating website, I was
shocked to hear that he had killed her after six
months of dating, leaving her young children behind. I
was considering at that time to start looking at online
dating but hearing and reading that story knocked the
idea right out of my head. It was a difficult place to be.
On the one hand, I liked dating - meeting a man,
going out for dinners, having fun while on the other
hand, and the safety of my children came first. If I
wanted to buy a car I could go to a website, search for
a particular model and make but then I asked: why
couldn't there be a website where we could check out
the man, we are about to date?

 Once, one man I met tried for weeks to invite me to
his home but I refused because I was scared. I kept
telling myself he could be a rapist, abuser or
murderer; these thoughts would run through my mind,
leaving me even more worried. I tried checking him
out via social media but I found nothing. There was
nowhere for me to go and after speaking with a few
single parents I found out that they felt the same way.
None of them wanted to bring a man home, only to

find out later that he was someone from hell. In the end, I did not allow this man to collect me from my home and whenever we had met, I was the one who drove to the meeting place. I always ensured we meet in public places and though he ticked most of the boxes for what I was looking for, he turned out to be a man who kept requesting me to buy him things.

We really had nothing in common and the sad thing about this was he was the first man I had met in ages whom I wanted to get serious with. I was ready for him, ready to love again and for love to be returned. I wanted to share my life with him but he turned out to be Mr. Wrong. Unfortunately.

The way I looked at it, I knew I was an excellent person with a great sense of humor, friendly and easy going, with a great business mind who lived with my son and not struggling in any way. Because of this, I knew the right man would eventually reveal himself and those things made me proud.

I had worked very hard to get to where I wanted to be and now when my children and me do go on holidays, we have the best life has to offer. Some men have felt intimidated by my independence since they think I may not need them as I already take care of myself; thus, they feel they have nothing more to offer. For me, any man who wished to be in my life just needed to be themselves - helping and supporting me whenever and however they could. I may have a nice home, a nice car and pay my own bills but I am still a woman who would like to be with a man to share my life with, I would like someone who should be able to take care of me and I, him.

What are my requirements?

- He must be of a certain age

- Sharing the same spiritual goals

- Single with all children grown up - if he has any.

- He must have his own home.

- He must be working/self-employed

- He must know what he wants in life.

- Must like going out traveling.

- Must treat me with respect.

- He must take care of himself and know who he is.

- He must be caring and patient.

- He must be tall, good looking.

I could go on and on with my list about what I am looking for? I too must be prepared to meet and allow this man to be who he is and not put all my expectations on him.

TIP:

There is nothing wrong with having a list. What are your requirements when seeking your ideal partner?

"What's Required For You?

What's Required For Me?

Let's Meet In The Middle!"

DATING AS A SINGLE MUM

As a single mum, trying to date can be so difficult since some of the men you so happen to meet think you were either desperate or felt your options in finding a man were 'limited'. Some men think the best thing that could ever happen to you was meeting them and yet others would want to treat you as their personal booty call - if you allowed them. Some wished to stay long enough to know you and your children, when all you really wanted was for them to stay for one night but they in turned would wish for more booty calling nights.

As a lone parent you know you cannot go down that road since you do not want your children to see too many men coming and going from your house, more so your bedroom. As a lone parent you think only of protecting your children, making sure nobody abuses them and that could mean you being alone but in the end.

After my younger son's father walked away for the second time (he was 9 years old at the time), I focused on bringing him up and starting a new business. Now, he is 18 and for those past nine years, I have been very lonely. I wanted to go on dates but was fearful as I did not want men to take advantage of me; they tended to feel I needed them more than they needed me. Furthermore, I did not want to pick any man who wanted to be kept, coming to sit on my settee, taking over my TV especially as I paid the bills in the end. It was not worth the hassle and I just stayed by myself, bring up my son.

I got asked out a lot but I turned it down for fear of being abused, be it myself or my son, or what if he turned out to be a man from hell. When my youngest son became18 years old, doing his own thing, I was ready to go on dates again; since he could take care of himself and I do not need to worry about him anymore. The funny thing though, both   of my young men would ask me questions whenever I am going out on a date:

"When are you coming home?" "Who are you going with?"

"Make sure they bring you home on time."

It would seem the roles have been reversed!

Recently, I went on a date but I was finding it very difficult to continue as the rules of the dating game had changed. On our first outing, he spoke of the kind of person he was and how he had not been with a woman for a long time since he was waiting for the right one. He said he was looking for a long-term relationship and that sounded good.

One day, he invited me to his place (he lived outside London). At first, I did not want to go but finally said "okay". I must say, he was good. He cooked and I felt relaxed. Afterwards, he wanted us to go shopping and took me to a camping shop since he was going camping soon. When we got there, he asked me to buy him a tent!

At first, I thought he was joking and stared at him like really? Are you serious? What are you saying? Are you kidding me?

I was so shocked; I could not believe that this man was asking me to buy him his tent. Even when he looked at me and asked: "Are you going to buy it for me?"

I was appalled by his behavior and immediately knew that this relationship was not going to work (even though I wanted it to) and after three months of dating him, I walked away. As much as I wanted to stay with him, to see if we could work things out, I knew it would not work. At the back of my mind, I kept thinking he was mean and I really wanted better for myself. I had waited so long for Mr. Right to come I would not allow any man to come and treat me like "Miss Money Bags." The bottom line being I was tired of kissing frogs hoping one day one of them would turn into my knight. I refused to kiss any more toads.

TIP:

Being a single mother does not stop you from being beautiful, desirable, sensuous, and sexy. Never stop caring and looking after you. Your Prince will appear when you are ready.

"I've dated from single to married back to single and it's all been enlightening!"

My First True Love

I love my first son's daddy very much!

When we first met, he was on the stage on tour with his band from America; they were playing all their latest music. When they stopped playing, my friends and I could not stop clapping and cheering. Then, all of a sudden, this man was in front of me playing his guitar and dancing. I stopped and looked at him before turning away and dancing with my friends but he came right in the middle of our group and began dancing again. Eventually the music changed to a slow song and suddenly, I felt his handgrip mine as he pulled me towards him. He was smiling as if he finally had me and was not going to let me go. Holding me very close, I tried pulling away, but he just smiled, holding me even closer. When the song came to an end, he introduced himself to me with an American accent, hoping I would be impressed - I was not! In addition, for the rest of the evening, he followed me around until I gave him my phone number. I said to myself, "He is not going to call by 8:30am; he must be crazy if he do!

The next day 8:30am, my house phone rang and I thought to myself, "Who is calling at this time of the morning?" with my head thumping from drinking too much the night before as I fought with the phone.

"Hello." I said, recognising the American accent. "Oh! It's you. What do you want?"

"I am calling you so that I can take you for breakfast or lunch."

I replied, "I don't eat breakfast." "Then I'll take you for lunch." He said. "I don't eat lunch."

"Okay, I'll take you for a drink and don't tell me you don't drink because I know you do. You may as well say yes. Otherwise, I'll keep you longer on the phone."

I said "yes" and put the phone down. It rang again shortly after.

"Meet me at 7:30pm. How will I know you will come?" He asked.

"Yes, I'll be there."

When I got there, I was thinking to myself: What am I doing coming out here? Maybe he was ugly, but when I saw, him and he smiled, I said to myself: He is good looking.

We went out for three years before he returned to America and by the time, I was about four months pregnant, and he did not want me to come to the airport with him. Therefore, for the entire day I stayed home in bed, crying my eyes out. It was a horrible day! My flat felt cold and empty even though it was summer.

With the support of my friends, I went through the pregnancy, but that experience was one of - the loneliest days of my life!

I was young and not ready to be a mum and thought I couldn't look after myself more so a baby. As the months went by my friend's phone calls became less and less, I grew more and more depressed, and lonely, worrying about how I was going to bring this child up on my own. I found comfort in writing poetry about our love and how much I missed my ex - my lover - the potential father.

Those were tough days and very lonely nights raising a child; while the man I love was so far away!!

How could I ever love again?

TIP:

You will always love but always, always, remember to love yourself first.

"You Never Forget That One True Love"

REMEMBER

Remember me, as I do you, with the loving tenderness, that we had for one another. Remember the affection,

The warmth that we were able to give, Each other.

Remember the kind words; we used to say to each other.

The feelings we had when we touched each other; When we walked through the park, listening to the birds singing the sweet melody, the songs of lovers.

Remember the times we walked in the rain; Laughing, talking, and dancing as if we had no problems, In the world.

Just as in love but also remember, the bad times that we had.

"In the mind is where the stories always stay"

MISS YOU

I miss you, now, as always.

I know that the time spent with you is not time enough,

there can never be enough time for us. Though we are not together.

I still remember the early mornings, waking up, still hugged up from the night before, and you, still asleep.

I remember how I would slip out of bed; to make you coffee, but I am now alone. I Miss You!!

Time has stood still for me.

Days and nights have become longer and longer, all blending into one.

Perhaps, this is selfish.

I know, but what is selfish? When all I wanted to do was, to spend every moment with you.

Every dream, our dreams, every hope, our hope:

Hopes and plans to share our lives together. Every breath we took was our life.

My life was created to love you.

You completed my life just by you loving me. When I think of the afternoons, it is autumn or perhaps spring.

When I think of you, you remind me of the fine summer wine and the warmth that comes from deep, within your heart.

You are my life, as the sun glows, the trees are green, that's when I know that you will be coming back to me soon.

Come soon my love; come back to me soon. I Miss You!

BORED

I sit there bored.

Counting the days, the months

When I would see you.

I don't feel like going out,

as long as you are not with me.

I don't feel like talking to friends!

OH! How bored I am sitting here!!

Every morning I go down stairs,

hoping to see a letter from you.

OH! Darling how bored I am

sitting here waiting to hear from you.

I get so disappointed when

I don't see a letter from you,

but I still go downstairs every morning,

hoping to find a letter by the door.

I sit here lonely and bored,

realising that it's not the friends we have,

nor the places that we used to go,

made me happy. It's you.

TAKE MY HEART

Take my heart and fill it with love; Take my cold nights and warm them, gently, with loving tenderness.

Take my love and caress it into your loving hands.

Take my lonely days and fill them; with laughter, joy and happiness. Take my bitter and empty evenings;

turn them into joyful, memorable nights. I will give all that is mine to get you.

"A heart is a delicate organ, handle with care"

FEELINGS

What a great thing it is:

to be able to feel, to see and have our souls joined,
For life.

My feelings for you grow stronger every day.

Oh! Darling how I miss feeling the softness of your
body.

How it used to turn me on, Made my eyes shine in the
dark.

Oh! How I miss feeling the firmness of your body.

How it used to make me feel, like a woman.

Oh! How I miss feeling your strong arms around my
naked body. How it used to make my breasts stand
up, made my legs go weak, me flopping down on the
bed.

 The feeling of your chest on my chest; how it used to
make me feel dizzy with love. Oh! Darling how

I miss the feeling of your body; as you kissed me and
caressed me, how it made me feel like I was in
heaven. Oh! Darling, I miss your love.

"Having The Right Attitude Will Open Many doors Of Opportunities.

Having The Wrong Attitude Will Also Close Those Doors Too"

THE BURNING FLAME

The light burns furious, without love; so carelessly without any feelings, so bright, yet, with the hatred of life. So empty and sad;

I watched the light die out, without the reflection of your face. In my heart; the light burns so soft, like a candle.

The embers of our love that we shared together.

Remember the affection the warmth that we were able to give, to each another.

MENTAL UNIVERSE

Our mental universe I am there with you, though not in body, though not in body

But my heart and soul, is there with you always.

Each wall that you looked at in your room; I am there, standing against it, asking you to touch me. So deeply and tender: with the love that says: I care for you! a pure love, that is waiting to be caressed by you.

Each piece of furniture in your room; that you hold, you are holding me closer to you, until our heartbeat as one.

Our souls wrapped as a three-corded rope that cannot be broken.

Our bodies submitting into, our mental universe that bonds us together into passionate lovemaking.

Our private world:

Our mental universe, that ties us together as one; until the end of our days.

"Let the fire burn in my heart and soul"

THE SINGLE MUM'S POEM

I need a person in my life!

Because not everything we single, parents can do ourselves. We need hugs and kisses, other than from our children.

I need adult conversion to break my daily routine; someone I can download on, when things gets tough.

I need a person, who will ask me how my day was, and they will listen to me, encourage me,

And I will do the same for them.

"Being a single parent and mother is my badge of honour"

LIFE AS A TEENAGE MUM

When I become pregnant at an early age and the man that I truly loved returned to New York, I was completely heartbroken. I did not know how I was going to cope without him. My heart ached about the future. There were so many questions going around in my head and I kept crying all the time. I could not sleep nor eat and that made me lose weight to the point even my doctors were worried about me.

I was lonely and with all my friends still enjoying their youth, I was seeing them less and less as my stomach grew and grew. I was finding it hard to move around and walking became difficult with my back always aching and my feet getting as big as an elephant's. I would go to work, come home and just cry myself to sleep every night.

One day I stopped by a shop and bought some note pads and pens. I started writing poems because my friends were fed up with me talking about the father of my child and crying all the time. Then I wrote my first poem and began to feel better for the first time. I could express my fears without the feeling of being judged and I had discovered I could write.

Pouring my feelings onto those note pads gave me escapism from the world's darkness and loneliness and I began to learn more about myself, discovering my strengths and weaknesses. I also became more determined that I was going to make it for my unborn child. I was going to do whatever it took to make it.

Those were dark and lonely days as you can see in my poems. but now my eldest is an adult who has a family of his own. I am now a grandmother of six and we try to meet up every Sunday for dinner. I would say those dark days are behind me now with only happy ones ahead.

TIP:

Your life is not over if you are a teenage single mother, don't despair, you are more phenomenal than you think

"It never ends as long as you're alive, make the most if it!"

I Know Why the Caged Bird Sings

I was 21 when I went to see Maya Angelou at her book signing and reading: I Know Why the Caged Bird Sings.

I just had my older son and was filled with fear and many questions, how was I going to look after him since I was but barely a child and could hardly look after myself much less a baby who would need to depend on me for all his needs? I felt like that caged bird in that narrow cage who could not fly.

I asked, what was our future? What was in store for the both of us? A question I was unable to answer since my confidence was at its lowest point. I had felt rejected, ugly, helpless, and very sad. But as I listened to Maya read her poem, my eyes filled with tears and my heart filled with great sadness and confusion. In that moment as I fought the tears, I told myself I needed to stand up and not allow fear to defeat or control me. I was determined to make it because my son needed me.

At the book signing part, Maya autographed her book for the guests, and never once did she look up when asking the person's name and when it was my turn, I became nervous. She looked up at me, smiling and said: "Hey beautiful, what is your name?"

I replied: "Margaret."

She wrote, inside the book: "To my beautiful Margaret."

When I left that hall, I felt 6ft tall since nobody had ever called me beautiful before in my life. I held that book close to my heart since I knew it was down to me to be the savior for my son. I was in such a hurry and could not wait to get home to collect him from my neighbor. When I did, I kissed him as we made our way home, holding onto him so tight. I said: "We are going to make it," but he could not hear me since he was fast asleep!

Maya Angelou gave me the encouragement I needed with her warm smile and compassionate words. I may have felt like a caged bird before but when I left that event, I was a new person ready to take on the world and the challenges it held for me as a single parent.

The Poem: I Know Why

The Caged Bird Sings –

by Maya Angelou

The free bird leaps on the back of the wind and floats downstream till the current ends and dips his wings in the orange sun rays and dares to claim the sky.

But a bird that stalks down his narrow cage

can seldom see through his bars of rage

his wings are clipped and his feet are tied

so he opens his throat to sing.

The caged bird sings with fearful trill

of the things unknown but longed for still and his tune
is heard on the distant hill

for the caged bird sings of freedom

The free bird thinks of another breeze

and the trade winds soft through the sighing trees and
the fat worms waiting on a dawn-bright lawn and he
names the sky his own.

 But a caged bird stands on the grave of dreams his
shadow shouts on a nightmare scream

his wings are clipped, and his feet are tied so he
opens his throat to sing

The caged bird sings with a fearful trill

of things unknown but longed for still and his tune is
heard on the distant hill for the caged bird sings of
freedom.

"A successful businesswoman is strong, full of grace and wisdom, having a full understanding of her future and needs"

THIS LIFE

"I won't allow someone to master my emotions; I'll take control and be the leader of my destiny"

OH! THIS LIFE

What is there in life? When every corner, that I turn to is blank. The future looks empty; I get up in the morning, dreading to step into my small old shoes, next door,

 I can hear the kids screaming, yet, for a few seconds,

I blank my mind and transfer myself

to a different world of glamour and beauty; a world that is pure,

that holds nothing but love and affection, A world I should belong to.

The cold wind blows

against my face from the broken window. It brings me back to reality

The world that I don't want to face.

the world without a future,

 for me and my kids.

A world without love and kindness.

"I'm going to embrace my future as a single mother now and walk towards my destiny"

WHAT SORROW AWAITS ME

Daily tears follow what a world of sorrow they created little happiness. Why all this sadness?

What can I as a single mum do?

That is not bad?

And what can I do so

That the nation will not be criticised.

 For there is no perfect person found in this world that we live in.

No hour ever passed without a pain.

No minute ever fades without a cry.

When shall all these ends?

MY SON

My son, where there is life; there you are,

You are the string of my heart; playing sweet melody inside me. You are my life:

my past, my future and present. My son, you are:

my strength, my courage, and my energy; to keep me carrying on,

when the going gets tough.

My son when I see you smile, laugh and dance, my heart would sigh, with the knowledge

that I have done my best bringing you up with love and happiness.

My son when you hug me and kiss me softly,

my heart would glow with love wiping away all the heartache of a parent

My son I am so proud of you! As I watched, you grow,

from childhood to manhood,

bearing all the qualities of a fine young man It makes me stand "11 ft." tall.

Looking down at you;

smiling, praising, and encouraging you, to do your best.

My son, I love you!

"If you love money, you'll never be satisfied. If you long to be rich, you'll never get all you want"

HAPPY BIRTHDAY MY SON

My son

today you are two years old!!

I wish you all the happiness

that the world can give you.

At every corner which you take, let there be a bright light shining on you,

Let there be happiness at every step that you take, my son.

Happy Birthday, my Son.

"Love your children forever; they'll be better for it"

I Am Proud Of You My Son

My son; how proud I am as I watched you, letting your hand try to touch me. How proud I am to watch you grow to a sweet young man.

With all the qualities that are required for a young handsome man.

How proud I am to hold you close to me as I hear you cry.

My heart fills with the joy of happiness: Knowing that you are part of me.

To look at you;

to see how you have changed my life. You made me want to be alive,

you filled my heart with such happiness; a love I never knew.

How proud I am to watch you sleep, so quietly. How I loved to stroke the softness of your cheek.

My Son! How proud I will always be.

THE CHALLENGES

"I must never give up no matter what life throws at me because winners never quit"

There were some challenges I faced as a single mum when trying to date and raise my children. Ranging from managing finance, childcare, lack of support from friends and family, time for self, keeping the children entertained, seeking employment or setting up a business, introducing my children to a new partner and the social isolation; these were just a few of the problems. I know that these challenges were not unique to individuals and some of you reading this book may think: 'Ha ha! You have narrowed it down to only few points. In all fairness, single mothers face many issues on a daily basis, starting in the morning, when we wake until we go to sleep.

THE FINANCIAL STRAIN

After running my business for several years, I was doing well financially - paying my mortgage, bills and being able to purchase a second house. I was so proud of myself in achieving so much as a single mum. However, I paid a high price for that since I had to close the door to dating since I did not want a man to take away my focus by becoming a liability to me and not be a positive role model for my son. Neither did I want to go around picking up after him and paying all the bills as he would probably be unemployed. This had happened so many times to the few men I allowed into our lives as I kept saying, I had a man at home. But eventually, I was unwilling to carry any man that was not part of my plan as I moved to achieve my own goals and with everything going really well, I did not want to be unsettled.

My new retail business allowed me to travel and go on holidays. It was doing well. I was financial secured until 9/11 happened and after six months, my business went downhill since it depended on importing merchandise from overseas like America, Turkey, Cyprus, Italy, and France. After 9/11, I couldn't travel as often as I would like and after a year of struggling to keep the business open, I made the heartfelt decision to close the shop. It was another heartbreaking time, and I cried all the time, I had worked so hard to build my business as well as being the sole provider for myself and my children. Those times were financially very difficult. After I closed the business, I was in a confused state. I couldn't focus on anything, not even my own children's needs.

Questions flooded my mind all at once: how was I going to pay my bills, my mortgage or even put food on the table?

How would I find a job – my biggest challenge?

Who would employ me? Especially since I always worked for myself.

Those questions opened a big door of worries and I sunk into a state of depression with more crying and anxiety attacks. Visiting the Job Centre to sign on was not an option! So, I sat down and had a long think about, how was I going to bring money into the house? I looked at my savings, all I had was £6,000. I knew I could not live the carefree life I once had and had to change the way I felt, thought about money, used, and spent it. I had to learn how to budget. I also knew I had to return to college to retrain myself, so that I had a better chance in getting a job which would sustain myself and my children.

I remembered one morning, after dropping off my youngest at school, I went into the bank to get an up-to-date bank statement and that morning and afternoon, I sat trying to put a budget together. I was determined to make the

£6,000 last the entire year while I returned to college and retrained. At this point my older son had left home and it was just me and the younger one.

I remembered budgeting £18 a week to live on. Those were very, very difficult times for myself and my children. An isolating period too since I could not afford to go out with my friends. I felt left out and the little money I had was to treat my son, including planning a good day out for us. I must say I did have the right support from my family, where my sisters and brother would help during the school holidays by having my him for the odd weekend, giving me respite - like staying in bed a little late some days. There were times when I had no food in the house and worried about how I was going to feed my son. One day, I sat crying when my phone rang. It was my cousin who worked as school caterer. She said she would be home at about five o'clock and that I should come by to collect some food. I picked up my son from school, gave him some dried toast then drove to my cousin. She had cooked and offered me some groceries, and what she gave us lasted for a month! I explained to her what I was going through, and she assured me she would ensure we always had food in the house.

I never ever asked my son's father for anything, no matter how difficult things were with me.

But one day, things were really bad, and I did not have any money to buy milk for our son. I did not have anyone else to ask and I did not like borrowing money from friends. It was not something I ever had to do since I felt that could mess up a great friendship. So, that day, I decided to call my sons' father for some money. At the beginning of the conversation, he was okay until I asked him for £5. Suddenly he was making fun of me. I started crying. At the time, I was at a friend's house and she heard me crying. She took the phone, put it down, and said: "I will give

you the money. Don't you ever call him again! You deserve better."

That was the last time I ever spoke to him and or over nine years he had just disappeared until one day I bumped into him in a shop.

I stared at him, as he looked rough, not the good-looking man I once knew. He kept saying to me that I looked good. I guess I did since I had just finished college and found myself in a great job mentoring families and disadvantaged kids - how cool was that?

Today, I am back running my own business and happy with my life!! I'm not quite there yet but I am not where I was before, changes I made in my life and mind-set, meant:

Learning how to budget and control my money. Therefore, making tough decisions and organising how I handled my finances.

I made sure to do monthly shopping and to do so when my son was at school (thus helping me avoid buying things I had not budgeted for).

I tried very hard to stick to my monthly budget, though; it did not work sometimes because of unexpected bills.

I needed a financial plan that would help me manage my finances.

Little holidays, Christmas, rainy days, and I saved every month for school uniforms.

When I started working this was the system,

I used to help me stay on top of my finances.

SOCIAL ISOLATION

At times, I felt trapped underneath a lot of responsibilities and unable to cope with the daily routine laid before me. Sometimes this left little time to go out on dates or quality time with my friends. Sometimes it left me lonely with the same questions time and time again: when would this road, filled with loneliness end? When would I be able to meet my Mr. Right?

The feeling of loneliness and fear created a barrage of uncontrollable negative thoughts and at times, my self- esteem would hit rock bottom, especially when bills needed to be paid at the end of a month. There were times I longed for a loving and intimate relationship, but it seemed so far away especially as I always tried to put my children first. I did not get it right all the time since no A-Z book existed on how to bring up children.

I remembered one day my younger son was going to school by himself and I followed the bus all the way to school in my car. I asked myself, what was I doing? Why was I following the bus? Pulling into a car park, I sat there and cried my eyes out. I felt a bit redundant as my school running days were ending. (I was so used to him being with me in the car and walking him to the school gate, how I suddenly would feel lonely inside, when I watched him walk away). That day after work, on my way home, I began to think I now had to start getting a life for myself and prepare for the time when my son will leave home. So, I started going out more, building a network of friends. I would look for places where I could go and socialise with other mothers. I would also look for play schemes and after school activities for my son to attend.

Once a month, I went out for dinner or on a weekend with some friends and these little steps helped me to rebuild my confidence and reduce the isolation.

DECISION MAKING

I loved being carefree!

I hated making decisions or having to worry about the lives of others since I knew my decisions could impact greatly on their lives, good or bad. Things happened in life; like gaining a job, lifestyle change or a sudden trip and if I

 wanted a new dress or shoes, one did not have to consider or think of anyone else but themselves. In those days my decisions affected only me. Making decisions as a single parent was a different thing, there were no set rules, instructions or directions for raising children parenting can be hard with a lot of grey areas and as a single mother you do not have another adult to talk things over or to share with.

With my last son becoming a teenager, I started meeting other parents I could bounce thoughts and ideas off, share fundamental values or receive advice. Even then, the toughest parenting decisions I had to make at the time were around whether to ground him for months, say no; stop him from being with his friends, going out to parties or just going out for fun.

As a single parent, like any other parent, I have made mistakes, felt guilty about them too. Nevertheless, not being afraid to correct the problem has helped me to be a better person.

I have learnt not to be too hard on myself since I cannot fix the past; instead, I focus on making the next   day a better one. Nowadays, I put my focus and energy into being a better person.

"I've the option if I fall, to either get back up or keep on going or to stay down. When I choose to keep going, I discover more of what life has for me"

MY CHILDREN MAY BE JEALOUS OF A NEW PARTNER

Many single parents entered the role via various scenarios: personal choice, divorce, separation or death of a partner and we all face similar challenges. Any man who dated a single mother would have to be very courageous because as a single parent we come with a different set of rules where our children must be factored into any decision or role the man would like to play. Dating for a single mother, usually took a back seat when the need of her children comes first. This may be problematic for a single mother as well as the man they planned to date or are dating. So, the man who comes along have to love children, have lots of patience, be caring, understand and be sensitive to the needs of a ready-made family.

It would be a big worry whenever we dated a man willing to fit in with the family, but the children tend to be jealous and usually would like to have their parents to themselves. They can be resentful and may not want to share their parent's affections with anyone else. Most of us tend to be concerned about our children's feelings of jealousy, whereas the child/children may feel scared since they think their mum or dad no longer loved them. In itself that may create problems.

I remembered this guy who really liked me.

He was a handyman and I called on him at whenever anything went wrong in the house. He was very good with my young son, buying him toys and playing with him when he visited. One day he decided to visit as a friend and not as a handyman. On most evenings, I do not allow any visitors I do not really know into my home but this weekend the doorbell rang, and it was him. I was not expecting him, and my son asked who he was. I told him. He stopped playing with his toys and walked with me to open the door and I led our visitor into the sitting room. He was well dressed and had a bottle of wine in his hand. My son pushed by me, walked up to him, and asked: 'Why are you all dressed up? Are you going to take my mum out and why are you wearing women shoes? Mum he's wearing woman shoes and smells like he's wearing women's perfume!'

I told my son to be quiet and asked the man to sit, he gave me the wine and I asked if he wanted a glass. He said yes. I went into the kitchen expecting my son to follow like he always did but he did not. He just stood in middle of the sitting room watching our visitor as if he was a total stranger. Our visitor tried having a conversation with him but my son was not having it. Normally they would play silly games together but this time my son was not in the mood. When I returned to the sitting room, my son wasstill standing in same place. I handed our guest a drink and I sat. My son came, sat on my lap, and would not move. After a while our guest rose to leave without finishing his wine. At the door, he wanted to kiss me on my cheek when my son called: 'Mum its cold, close the door!'

Our visitor left and I closed the door. Taking my son's hand, we returned to the sitting room, and he went back to playing with his toys like nothing had happened. I asked him why he had done that, he said he did not like our guest and hoped he did not come back. That was the end of that conversation.

As a single parent we have little time on our hands and it must be spent wisely. Most times dating was not a priority since our days tend to be full of commuting, son's homework and juggling numerous other tasks. When we do squeeze in a relationship, we have to ensure it was healthy for us and our children. I tried maintaining a social life with the hope I may meet a loving partner who my children would accept.

I felt I was ready to date, energised and motivated by friends when I met a man, we exchanged numbers and began talking. He seemed really nice, and I told him I was a single mother with an eight-year-old son. He seemed okay with it. I asked him to call me at nine or ten at night since by then my son would be in bed, dishes washed, toys put way and schoolwork finished for the following day. Once those were done, I was able to have a conversation without any interruptions.

It was nice hearing a male voice asking how my day was and I looked forward to his calls. We spoke for a few weeks and arranged to meet up one day for a drink. He agreed but when the time came, he never showed or phoned. I called him a few times but he never picked up or responded, so I left the venue. Two days later, he called and apologised.

 Then one late evening he asked me to visit his home for a drink, I told him I could not at that, time plus I did not know him well enough to visit, and I had nobody to care for my sleeping son. He went quiet, I said bye and hung up. That was the last time we spoke.

I was upset for days but I knew I needed to be strong for my son. I must admit, every evening I missed that male voice over the phone.

As time went by my self-esteem would be lower since friends kept asking me how it was with the new man in my life but I was too ashamed to tell them it was over; most times avoiding the question or changing the subject. It was very difficult being single and dating and got even harder as a I became a golden ager.

"I would love my children no matter what – single or with a partner"

Embracing Happiness as a Single Parent

Today, dating can be hard because the good old days of how to do so has gone out the window. Say, you go out with your mates for a good girly night out, you were chatted- up, bought a drink, flirted, and laughed with, the guy hoping that by the end of the night you would exchange numbers. Nowadays, everything was via the internet like online dating. Some of my friends have asked me about going online to date but I refused to go down that road. I am so scared of meeting a man who would be trouble or worse. There have been too many horror stories.

When I was young and dating, I was full of confidence, I knew what I wanted on a date and in men but now at my age, it has become very difficult, not only time consuming but would my sons accept this new man in my life. Often now, when I get dressed to go out, they ask questions like:

"Where are you going?"

"When are you coming home?"

"Whom are you going out with?"

"Are you driving or are they coming to pick you up?"
"What time did you come home?"

I told them to stop asking me questions since they were not my husband. Once, when going on my first date after nine years, I was so sacred and went online to check this guy out. He was not on any of the social media platforms and that worried me. On the day of the date, I gave my sons the details of the guy.

As a single parent, I found there was no time for me to think about my happiness but now I can put my happiness first and go on holiday by myself and did so for the first time in many years. At first, I was nervous and had asked my son to come with me but he said no, he wasn't coming - so I went by myself instead an absolutely loved it. I was not worried about him and slept in most days until late. Importantly, I did whatever I wanted to do – it was a "ME Time", for sure.

I am now learning to embrace my newfound happiness as a single parent. However, it would still be scary going out on holidays without my son but I have made up my mind to take short breaks around the outskirts of London to build my confidence by doing things without my children. It took a while to be out there again but now I am, I follow a new set of rules:

Believing in myself since I am beautiful inside and outside

Believing, loving, and trusting in me believing in my first instinct, never settling for anything less. If it did not feel right, I will not go there.

Be comfortable with the person

Whomever I am going to date, I must feel comfortable with that person and ensuring my safety came first, even if it meant exploring the relationship further. I must be very clear in what I want in a relationship and the kind of man I want to bring home to meet my family and friends.

Be upfront

Fully disclosing about me being a single parent with two grown boys and the youngest living with me.

Set my standards high

As a dating single parent dating the stakes were higher since I have to remember that it was not all about me anymore and whoever I invited into my life must be truly worthy of me *and* my children.

I will watch out for the red flags

On my last date I missed the red flags. I recalled one where I was invited to dinner but never asked where we were going. So I went overdressed and the fact that he had eaten already. He kept talking about money and on our fifth date, took me to a shop asking me to buy him an expensive item. What I did not say was he had said his car needed petrol. At this point, I just closed my ears and after a few dates, I said goodbye. He had looked, sounded so good, and yet was so Mr. Wrong.

ME TIME FOR ME

I found myself very exhausted by the end of the
evening or as the weekend approached, my energy
levels would be low because of the many things I had
to complete; like dropping my son at friends, home to
clean, wash, iron and food shopping before rushing
out again to pick him up. Worse if he had to attend a
party. Without having the fathers of my sons involved
or a partner as a role model, I had to rely on family
and friends. Sometimes when my   sons were asleep
I would go and pour myself a glass of

 wine, select a book and go into a corner of the sitting
room, creating my 'me time'.

I also created a network of other single mothers to
assist. We would rely on each other so that we could
do things that needed to be done. Sometimes I felt
the weekends were way too short because by the end
of Sunday, Monday school run, and work starts all
over again. My sons depended on me for everything
and making sure I   was responsible for all aspects of
their well-being was a priority, the only way I could
sustain the energy for this job was to create pockets
of "Me Time", when I could truly be in touch with
myself, holding onto   my individuality.

ENJOY BEING ME

I enjoyed being me because I am wonderful, beautiful and unique.

I enjoy being me because at my golden age, I am full of life.

I enjoy being me because I have so much to give back to others.

I enjoy being me because I have so much to look for in life and the brighter future that is head of me.

I enjoy being me because my children are all grown up and I do not have to worry too much about them.

I enjoy being me because I am now free to be me.

I enjoy being me because I no longer apologise, for my children's mess.

I enjoy being me because I have learned to accept myself, that I am wonderfully created and loved.

I enjoy being me because I love myself,

I enjoy being me because I am who I am

TIP:

Learn the eight; Let them be your everyday affirmation.

"I enjoy and love me always"

MY 14 TIPS ON HOW I CREATE ME TIME

I Get Up Early In the Morning

I would rise two hours before my son, go downstairs and make myself a cup of tea, return to my bedroom, listen to smooth soft music, read my favourite book for an hour, write a bit in my journal, look at to-do list book and start planning my day. I would road map my day and found this very helpful since it stopped me from being stressed before the day began. Those few minutes I spent in the shower before I woke my son was Me Time and by the time I left the shower, I was very clear on what I had to do to have a smooth and happy morning for the both of us.

My Bedtime Routine

It was very hard to put a bedtime routine in place, I worked on a plan to implement and ensured I was consistent until my son was used to it. Eventually he learnt to fall asleep in his own bed and that gave me enough room in my own to have a good sleep and rest.

I Give Myself at Least One Evening Off or Make a Date

As I put my son to bed, I would read him a bedtime story and kissed him good night, I would go make a hot bath, pour a large glass of wine, and jump in the bath with soft music in the background. I would gently sip my wine and think about how my day was, and then drift into a world of peace and joy. There were times I would use this moment to plan, daydream and reconnect with friends. By the time   I came out of the bath and into bed, I would feel rejuvenated and ready for the school run or work for the next day. Once a month I would also make a date with myself, go and purchase some energizing aromatherapy products I loved and all of the above with the added sexy negligee, glass of wine and a good book.

I WRITE DURING MY LUNCH HOUR

There was a time when I was fed-up with one of my jobs, I felt over worked, underpaid, stressed out, not liking my work and wanting to leave, but I knew I could not just walk   out without going into other. However, I really did not want to work for anyone else and I got tired of listening to my co-worker's shortcomings in the staff room. Then I   started taking short walks during my lunch break to clear my head and decided on what kind of business I wanted to set up. After which I then used my lunch break to meet with business advisers who helped me to write my business plan and before long, I had a training company and was employing staff.

A Quality Time for My Son and Myself

After I picked my youngest from school, cooked dinner, ate and helped him complete his homework I would get him to choose a DVD or TV programmes for us to watch. We would cuddle on the sofa, laughing and joking. If he were really good, we would celebrate with a trip to the library, park, museum or movies.

HOW I MAXIMIZE MY COMMUTING TIME

After dropping my youngest, I would put on a smooth jazz CD or gospel to relax me. I found this helped when responding to the challenges I faced at work, keeping me calm and not to over-react.

ACTIVITY DAY

There were days when I did not have money to go out with my youngest and I would collect his toys such as Play-doh, special markers and activity books and invite over my next door neighbor's child for him to have someone to play with. This gave me a few hours to catch up with the washing, changing bedspread etc. We would rotate the days with my next door neighbor, cutting his boredom.

Re-tour Household Chores

One day a week, I would get my youngest to participate in the chores. His job was to vacuum and tidy up his toys, wash dishes with me, tidy his bedroom and clean the bathroom. Now older, he still vacuumed the house every Saturday and helped keep the house clear and tidy. I must say both my boys can cook and keep a house tidy.

Going Out With My Friends

It was very difficult sometimes going out with friends especially when money was tight. It was not nice depending on them to pay for me. If I knew I was going out with my friends in two or three months, I would put a little bit of money away every week and by the time, the date arrived, I would have enough money saved. This made me confident in knowing I did not have to depend on anyone.

Loving Myself

My journey as a single parent taught me to love myself and stop feeling guilty about my sons' not having a father as a role model. It taught me to stop blaming others for my own shortcomings and to act in order to make life   better. I tried not to worry about things that I could not change nor control, changed, and controlled those things I could.

Balance Work and School Runs

Bringing up my two boys, I learnt very quickly to say "no" a lot, even though there were tears, screaming and kicking. I had to priorities and re-priorities, always ensuring the most important things stayed the most important and were completed first. It was a struggle balancing the days and weeks initially since I could not get everything right or to fall in place. There were times I was more family-focused and I knew what to do. Other times I did not have a clue and felt lost. There were times I was more focused on business and did not do my best to always ensure my boys were as comfortable and happy as possible.

MY LOVE FOR MY CHILDREN IS MY SHIELD

When I stopped speaking with the father of my children, it affected me very badly, but I stood strong and did not allow the negativity to stop me from achieving my goals. I thought about all the bad treatment I had received from men and was determined to work   hard so that the negativity would not hold me as a prisoner or stop me from meeting the man of my dreams. Therefore, to meet Mr. Right, I needed to be Mrs. Right, which meant dealing with my own baggage, ensuring that any new man who entered my life would not be like the men before. There are some amazing men out there, who know how to treat women right but they tend to be far and few in-between. I hope, one day I would find Mr. Right but in the meantime, I would use the time of being single to get prepared, be clear on what I am looking for and want from a man and manage my expectations.

 When I was young and dating, any man would do so long as he was good looking and sharply dressed. I did not need to know about his background or if he was the right one for me. He maybe he looking only for that booty call or a woman to provide a roof over his head as many men nowadays choose to do. Some men seek out a single mum because she has a house and a settled family. As a single mum, I could not keep making the same mistakes I made before and had learnt from my mistakes that good looks were not everything. Now, I look at the heart and watch his attention towards me.

My last experience confirmed that. After our third date, I finally invited him to my home, making sure my children were not around. He kept saying: "you have a big, nice house." Deep inside I kept telling myself: "you are not moving in since you are not Mr. Right but Mr. All Wrong."

KEY POINTS TO PREPARE MYSELF FOR DATING

To use love as the ultimate power in my life I must love myself and learn to do so as never before.

To fall in love with life again.

See only love, hear only love, speak only love and feel love with all my heart.

I must learn to leave bitterness behind me.

There is no limit, no ceiling to the amount of love you can feel, and it is inside me I am made to love the true man that is coming into my life.

To change the way I feel, from negative to a positive outlook on life and make a mental list on what I needed in a man.

My job was to love my children build a happy home for my children and myself.

I am going to make a conscientious effort to notice as many good things around me that I would like to share with my Mr. Right when he came along.

I have learnt to be grateful every day, giving thanks for my day. As a single mother, one could forget to stop and assess how our day had been or to take time for self and what was achieved in the day.

"ALWAYS BE YOUR EXCEPTION"

STILL I RISE

This poem was one of my anthems. I read it when the storms of life came, as they did in a various ways such as friends gossiping about me, particularly if I had loaned them money and they did not want to pay me back, being too fearful in making that first step in changing my situation and struggling to pay the bills. At times in need of a miracle, just to provide food, frustrated and worried about my children's future; confused, weary and helpless as there was no one I could turn to for help. Sometimes feeling heartbroken, rejected, and even defeated before the day even started. I felt discouraged by my youngest son school report and his behavior and kept asking myself how I was going to make it, turning the impossible to the possible. In this poem, I found so much confidence when things got really bad and I would read it out aloud and by the time I had finished, my confidence would be up and I was ready to take on the storms of life again.

Still, I Rise - by Maya Angelou

You may write me down in history with your bitter, twisted lies,

You may tread me in the very dirt but still, like dust, I'll rise.

Does my sassiness upset you?

Why are you beset with gloom?

Cause I walk like I've got oil wells Pumping in my living room.

Just like moons and like suns, With the certainty of tides, just like hopes springing high, Still I'll rise.

Did you want to see me broken? Bowed head and lowered eyes?

Shoulders falling down like tear-drops. Weakened by my soulful cries.

Does my haughtiness offend you? Don't you take it awful hard

Cause I laugh like I've got gold mines Diggin' in my own back yard.

You may shoot me with your words; you may cut me with your eyes,

You may kill me with your hatefulness, but still, like air, I'll rise.

Does my sexiness upset you?

Does it come as a surprise?

That I dance like I've got diamonds

At the meeting of my thighs?

Out of the huts of history's shame I rise

Up from a past that's rooted in pain I rise

I'm a black ocean, leaping and wide, Welling and swelling I bear in the tide. Leaving behind nights of terror and fear, I rise

Into a daybreak that's wondrously clear I rise

Bringing the gifts that my ancestors gave, I am the dream and the hope of the slave. I riseI rise I rise.

"I'LL ALWAYS RISE"

THE STORIES

"Every obstacle that presents itself is an opportunity to change things in your life"

MY MYSTERY STRANGER

One breezy summer evening I was going home from college. I was tired and hungry. As I walked slowly to the next bus stop, worried about the best route I could take to collect my son from the child-minder. Normally I needed two buses to get there but figured maybe I could walk the next two stops and that way, just have one bus to take. It would be a bit longer but at least I would save on money for tomorrow's journey. Ugh!! It's such a pain commuting without my car (which was in the garage, the mechanic taking forever to fix it!) I missed my ride since I really, I did not have the money to pay him. In addition, failing my English and shorthand exams was on my mind; I was in a pretty bad mood.

While walking pass a pub, someone called out to me. I did not answer and looked in the opposite direction. A man was shouting about inviting me for a drink, but I did not answer and he kept calling until I finally stopped, turning towards him. I said politely, "No thank you."

Deep down I wanted to tell him: "Go and get a life and stop bothering women as they passed by."

I continued walking, thinking, worrying; knowing full well, my fretting was not going to change my situation. From the corner of my eye I saw a car following me. It was a

Rolls Royce. It pulled alongside and the window rolled down. I was ready to hit the person with my books and scream for help and run, if he tried anything.

"So, you don't drink with strangers?" He asked.

"That's right. I don't know you therefore you are a stranger, and I don't drink with strangers," I replied and kept walking.

"Where are you going? Can I give you a lift?"

"No thank you, I do not get into cars with strangers," I answered.

"I'm not a stranger," he said.

"You are a stranger to me. Look, why don't you go and pick up your master, I'm sure you're running late and he's waiting for you."

"I don't have a master, I'm my own boss." He answered.

"Really, you expect me to believe you, a black boy like you driving a Rolls Royce. Okay show me your logbook."

"Okay, if I show you my logbook with my name on it, can I give you a lift to where you're going?"

He pulled across me. I stopped, still holding onto my books ready to hit and run. He opened his glove compartment and took out a logbook and for sure it had his name on it.

I then asked him to show me his driver's license. By the time I was through drilling him; I was so tired I just got into the car and true to his word, he took me where I wanted to go, (to collect my son). He also took me home, but I made sure he dropped me two doors away. He even asked for my number, but I refused to give it to him.

He said, "I tell you what, you take my number; when you're free, call me."

I replied, "I'll not be able to call just yet because I'm in the middle of exams."

"Call me when you're free." He repeated.

As he drove off, I stood waiting since I did not want him to know where I lived. I kept the card he gave me and wondered why it took me two months to call him but I did. I called wondering if he would remember me.

We talked and laughed, and I assumed he had not remembered me.

"Do you know who you're talking to?"

"No, I don't," he replied.

"How could you forget me so quickly? I was the lady you were trying to pick up and I was going to hit you with my books if you tried anything."

He laughed, "So you were really going to hit me with your books after I gave you a lift to pick up your son?"

"So, you do remember me?" I said.

"How could I forget; you gave me such a hard time. When are you free for me to take you out for dinner, at least you owe me that much?"

"I'm free this Saturday if you are," I said.

"Ok, I'm free Saturday, so I'll come and pick you up and please give me your right address. I know that where I dropped you off that day was not where you live. I saw you walking back with your son."

I gave him my home phone number and he called the following day. We ended up talking a lot before we even met for the dinner date and I was wowed when he came for me in his Ferrari. My mouth fell open when I saw it. And said to myself: "I've hit the jack-pot here!"

We went to a beautiful restaurant. He opened doors and pulled out my seat, making sure I sat first before he did. It seemed as if all the waiters knew him. It was a beautiful evening. We talked and laughed. He made me so   comfortable and right there our twelve-year relationship began, and the first three years were fantastic. But things changed.

He wanted a woman who stayed home, cooked and cleaned but I was not created for that, and over the next twelve years our relationship was on and off. I wanted to settle down and make a good go of our relationship.

Then, one day he said, "Let's go out for dinner, I want to talk to you."

I thought: 'Is he going to pop the question? Is he going to ask me to marry him after twelve years of an on and off relationship?'

I was so happy, I told friends he was going to propose that evening. I dressed beautifully, looked and felt it and was singing every kind of love song that popped into my head.

He collected me and we went to our favourite restaurant.

I was as excited as we ate and laughed and joked until we got dessert.

During that course, he said, "I have something to say to you."

But something was wrong and I knew it - did I want to hear what he had to say? Immediately I knew this had nothing to do with him asking me to marry him and that it was far, far worse.

Then he said and I heard: "I have a daughter with another woman, and she is three years old, I would like you to meet her."

He set down his fork, but I could not do the same, my mind was spinning, the hurt kicking in. I wanted to do something crazy, but my heart kept saying he was not worth it. I thought I had drunk too much as his words played in my head: 'I have a daughter; she is three years old and I would like you to meet her.'

I composed myself, trying not to look or sound like a fool, "Excuse me, what did you say?" I asked.

I wanted to be sure I had heard him right and he repeated the words. Suddenly I got up and went outside.

 I guess he paid for the meal since he followed me and for that very first time - I did not have any 'vex money' (emergency money should a situation or crisis arise on a date) for me to take a cab home.

 I got in his car with few words between us. When he pulled up outside my home, he asked, "Can I come in?"

I said no and got out of the car. He tried following but I stopped him. "Do not follow me inside if you know what's good for you. Let me advise you: get back into your car and go home because right now is not the time to talk to me."

I went inside, straight to bed and cried my eyes out. I phoned my child-minder and asked if it was okay for me to pick up my son the following day. She said it was.

After a few months of calling me, we agreed and planned that I would meet his daughter. But deep inside me, I knew I was not going to stay with him for much longer - it was time for me to say goodbye to my mystery stranger after 12 years of our loving relationship.

One day, he organised a day for me to meet his daughter and we went to a family event in a park nearby. His daughter was very beautiful, and she held onto my hand for the whole day. The day came to an end and he took his daughter home before returning to me. I thanked him for a wonderful time and told him I could not stay with him. I had to say goodbye and as I tried closing the door, he attempted to pull me toward him. He knew he had hurt me and I saw the pain in his eyes but he didn't know how to make it better for me - for us.

I stepped back and looked at him and said, "I love you but I cannot stay with you anymore. It's time for us to go our separate ways. You've hurt me too much and I don't think I could forgive you, so please, go." He looked at me as if to say: *'Are you sure this is what you want?'*

I looked away and opened the door for him to leave. As he walked away, I knew I would not see him again and my heart ached, the tears rolling down my face. You see, my pride, unforgiveness and bitterness, would not allow me to return to him, even though I loved him and wanted him back. Afterwards, he called many times, but I refused to pick up his calls and that was the end of a wonderful relationship.

TIP:

Wolves in sheep clothing, switch as quickly as can be; be careful, be aware.

"Each person comes with their own story, make sure you read the tale right"

GOODBYE - MY MYSTERY STRANGER!

Is there a light that comes on?

or is there a light that goes off, like a bus? When I am standing outside waiting for a bus: I would watch you walk by,how my eyes would follow you, until you disappear in the air,

and how I long for you to stop one day and talk to me. The cool breeze blew against my face;

so smoothly, how it reminds me of your soft brown eyes, as you stood across the road chatting to your friends, hoping you can look in my direction.

I shut down the outside world; in my thoughts,

there you lied down your smooth brown skin, in our private, spiritual world that is especially for us,

warm, full of kindness, forgiveness and love, for you and I.Nobody else exists for me but you;

I pick you out of the crowd, I tell you that you are the one, my heart has been searching for, and you are the one that my soul thirsts for, longing for your touch.

There is a light that comes and goes; there is a light that comes and goes, that light is you! Longing to touch you, holding you close to me nothing matters, at that moment but you.

My sweet, sweet.

Mysterious Stranger Good-bye!

"Goodbye can be final; it can also be temporary as life is"

YOUR FACE

Now you have gone.

Your face still lingering on like candlelight, It flickers but will never go out.

The warmth that the candlelight gives; it surrenders to the room,

Surrounding like a new birth of romance, so bright, so fresh.

Your image would always reflect on my mind, like a mirror.

Your face I would never forget.

"Images are like dreams; they stay if we want or go if we wish"

MEMORIES

There are many memories of you; because we were close, now you are away,

I feel lonely without you.

No matter how far away you are;

there will always be a very special place, in my heart for you.

"The heart is where you'll find the memory and there it'll stay"

THE FORBIDDEN FRUIT PART

There was a great man who told a woman not to eat a certain fruit; well, she ate the fruit and that was the beginning of the problems women face today with our men. These play out in our relationships and the pains we go through (like labour, love, pain, rejection, broken promises, and many, many more). I too, once ate from the forbidden tree.

My forbidden fruit came at night wrapped in beautiful red velvet. I knew I should not eat it, accept, or take it into my heart for I knew there were hidden dangers that could break me into a thousand pieces. I was young and full of life, wishing to try and have everything under my control but this particular fruit could never ever be fully mine nor could I ever tame it; unless, one day, it became completely and totally mine. Knowing all these things I still went ahead and ate, tasting its sweetness that brought short term happiness, laughter and joy and the feeling of being wanted.

Along the way I discovered myself by finding out how capable I was in loving a person and being there for them. This forbidden love awakened my soul and made me want more. Taught me never to settle for less in life or love. This forbidden fruit I gave my heart even though his was not mine to keep or to hold. I loved the way he made me feel whenever I was with him, sharing in jokes, laughing, going out and eating at top restaurants; that was exciting, but I was getting deeper and deeper into the relationship, I was hooked. He was like a drug that I could not stop taking even though I know the dangers that were ahead of me.

My forbidden fruit came every Wednesday, Friday, and every other weekend for passionate love-making, talking, laughing, making more love, and sharing special moments; later, it became like a burning candle, burning very softly in my heart, but I never told any of my friends, the pain and heartache I was carrying deep in heart; my false smile and laughter covering my heartache which I hoped nobody could see.

Wednesday wine bar night, I finished work early and soaked in the bath for hours, perfumed my body and chose black, white or blue underwear. I picked these colours because they brought out my best assets like my smooth dark shiny skin, waiting to be caressed and touched by my forbidden fruit. We would talk, gently kiss each other while drinking champagne and made steaming, passionate love all night. Even though he was my forbidden fruit, we were getting very close and deep in my heart I knew his hidden sword would one day pierce my heart.

We got to know each other very well and just hearing his footsteps, I knew whether we would have a night of passionate love making or just talk. Nevertheless, the time we gave each other was time stolen, time that did not belong to us, so at those precious times we tried not to waste them since we both knew the rules of the game we played and the outcome of our relationship.

One day, I remembered we were fighting over a chair; a high chair in my sitting room. I would sit on it whenever   he upset me since I felt that by sitting there, I would have more control and power being higher up, allowing me to speak down at him.

He looked at me and said, "Don't you think I know what you're doing when you sit on that high chair. Today you're not going to sit on it. We're going to sit on the floor together and talk."

We fought over the chair for nearly an hour.

He would get up and pull me down. He would sit on it and I would pull him down. This went on until we were both exhausted - that was the last time I sat on that chair – I learnt it was always best to talk things over with your partner, than play silly games.

The long awaited day I was expecting came and the sword swung, piercing my heart.

I knew all along I would need to let go since this forbidden fruit was not mine to keep but I could not bandage the wound or plaster the cut to stop the pain as it crushed my heart. With my entire body throbbing and aching at nights. My soul crying softly as I fell asleep. Who could I tell? Nobody knew because this love was top secret.

Only my forbidden fruit and I knew, and he needed to return to his rightful owner. Within me I knew my forbidden fruit would never again return to me.

My heart said: don't let go but my subconscious told me: you knew it was wrong and you still went there, let go and walk away. I told my subconscious: this is not the time for you to condemn me, comfort me and show me some kindness. Eventually rejection came knocking on my door, reminding me I was unworthy and would never find love like that again. So, I sought comfort in travelling the world since this was the only way I could move on.

Years later we met at a mutual friend's party.

I felt the love we once had but we both knew we would never take that risk again and though we were far apart, our love for each other still lived on.

Goodbye! Goodbye! My beloved forbidden fruit, I hope one day we meet again, maybe not in this lifetime. Farewell my forbidden fruit you came and taught me not to settle for less but to dare to dream my rightful fruit would one day come to me for me to hold and never to let go.

TIP:

Relationships whether casual or long term, will give or take a bit of you; sometimes it's forbidden, sometimes it's not and most times, it's hard to say goodbye.

"Sometimes it's not meant to be; live it, learn from it and keep moving"

FORBIDDEN FRUIT, I LOVE YOU!

I love you not only for what you are; but for what I am, when I am with you. I love you not only for what

You have made of yourself,

but, for what you have made of me. I love you for the wonderful things that you bring out of me;

when I am with you.

I love you because you understand me; when I am angry and unhappy.

How you would comfort me with a gentle kiss. I love you because you brought me out

Of my shyness; showing me the bright sun light of life.

How you made me look at things in a different way, than I ever did.

I love you because you helped me to understand myself; more than anyone has ever done.

You made me happy and relaxed:

 You have done all these by yourself, Perhaps, that's what it means been loved by someone.

Fibbing Fruit.

"The taste of the fruit is lingering; long may it stay"

LET ME BE THE ONE

"Let me be the one"; to comfort you, when you are down and out.

"Let me be the one"; to pick up the pieces,

when they have shafted, into thousands of pieces. "Let me be the one";

that cheers you up,

when you feel lonely and sad. "Let me be the one";

that answers all your questions. "Let me be the one";

that you tell your deep inner thoughts and fears.

"Let me be the one";

you chose to share

 your joy, happiness and sadness.

"Let me be the one"; that you come to when you need someone to empower,

motivate and be yours.

"I'll never be an option; I must be the priority"

LOVE MEANS

Love means; you don't have to say, "sorry".

Love means; to be kind to one another.

Love means; to feel, to see then again love stands; for So many meanings,

I can't explain them all. But I know one thing;

I love you; I love you.

"Let me love you, let it be forever"

FUN TO BE IN LOVE

It must be lots and lots of fun.

to be with someone that you love, knowing that they can make you happy and laugh, when you are blue

It must be fun to hear,

him saying, 'I love you' with a smile. That tells you he is telling the truth, it must be fun, when

he puts his hands around you.

Feeling the firmness of his body, saying; 'I care for you'

His brown eyes dazzling you with love.

"Laugh with love, let it be fun and love will smile"

THANK YOU FOR LOVING ME

I thank you; for all the goodness that you showed me.

I thank you; for the kindness, and honesty that you showed me.

I thank you; for the loving feelings, you always have towards me.

I thank you; for understanding my silly mistakes.

Oh! Darling! How I thank you; for a perfect relationship.

"To be in a loving relationship with one another, there's no better way but to be in love with one another"

JOY OF BEING LOVED

A love so full of happiness: so soft, like the falling of rain. So cool,

like a breeze that blows.

So gently, with the whisper of love, waiting to be touched. To be written in the form of a poem.

Born as free as a bird;

Sweet like music, so tender and gentle, like the mist of laughter.

Love that is so perfect, so still and calm,

like a pool of water.

Such love should remain untouched and undisturbed until the right time comes, for it to be woken by the right person.

"It's safe in joy, it's wonderful to be perfectly in love"

MR. DIAMOND DEALER

Where should I start with Mr. Diamond? I met him one Monday when I was selling diamonds at the time (I will not go into too much detail about my diamond business since that will be in my autobiography).

When I was introduced to Mr. Diamond by one of his friends, I told him I had diamonds to sell. He was sitting on a chair when he was speaking to me and my eyes were fixated on his good looks and smile. He was a very attractive man and this caught my attention. We started to   talk about him buying the diamonds while my heart and mind screamed: don't go there, he'll hurt you, he'll chew your heart up and spit it out. Not only that, men like him have women lined-up waiting for him to call on them, or he may have a wife tucked away waiting for him to come home night after night.

I told myself to step back, put him down and focus on the business. The last words I heard him say was he would buy the diamonds at half the price I bought them for. I stared at him, hard, and said no thank you. I cut the meeting short and walked away.

His shop was in the market, where I had my own stall and every time he walked by, he would stop and chat. Sometimes a conversation that held no interest to me. He would invite me for coffee or tea in his shop had I would always say yes but never went because I knew I was not going down that road with him.

In those days I did not spend the winter in the UK and right after New Year's Eve I would be away for three months. There was one year where I had not travelled, staying home for the first time in over four years. It felt strange and lost and lonely.

This year I needed to do an operation on my foot. He asked me out for a drink, and I said yes, and that was the beginning of my own downfall or where I fell for him, I would say. My heart screamed: 'don't do it, don't go for that drink' but I went to meet him anyway and we met in our local bar at the top of the market. As I walked in, his brown eyes lit up. He welcomed me with a kiss on the cheek and his smile and smooth voice got me as he introduced me to his friends, who were there too.

We talked and laughed and when I left the bar, I warned myself; 'do not cross that road, do not take him to your place, leave him where you found him'. Well, I did not listen to my own warning, and we met a few times. After I came out of hospital, he visited a few times, but I was walking away from the 12 year relationship and my poor heart still screamed: 'don't go there you're going down the wrong road, one filled with pain and heartache'.

My conscience spoke to me, stopping me as I was about to get into another relationship which could hold nothing but short-term happiness against a long-term one. But my physical and emotional self-will overruled my heart and conscience, and I went there. Our self-will and mind could be strong but if not controlled, could control us and that would be a bad place to be. Therefore, I allowed my self-will to step forward; it took me onto a dual carriageway I could not leave as I had come too far. By the time I did leave, I was battered and bruised by the storms of love. I had allowed my self-will to attract what I did not want. I had the power within to create a long lasting loving relationship and got what I expected to get from this one. Now I know I have power within me to create a successful relationship with others. I know I would one day have a loving relationship because my previous experiences have taught me to hold back and watch, exercise patience and love.

Therefore, I wished you all the best on your quest to finding the perfect relationship and I hope you enjoy the poem. 'My hope in life has given me the assurance of positive expectations'.

WHEN LOVE KNOCKS THE DOOR OF YOUR HEART

One evening love knocked on my door and asked me to follow. I did, though I knew his way was hard and steep and when he unfolded his wings, I yielded, despite the daggers hidden in them. Daggers that could hurt and yet I surrendered, and whenever he spoke I believed him since I knew his voice had power to shatter my dreams. Once his love covered me before exposing my shame and the pain living within, no room to hide. My heart would pound, filled with broken promises even though this love was for my growth and him, for my pruning.

Oh! Love holds a mirror up at me, magnifying my deeper, inner self. Love caresses me with tender loving, slicing open this poor heart of mine, unable to handle any more rejection.

Love! Love! He thrashes me until I am naked bearing nothing but my soul.

Love! Love! My dearest love, he sifts me like wheat, freeing me from my dehydrated hard heart to be a gentler loving person.

Love! Oh love! He squeezes me until I turn into liquid and then assigns me to a hidden place so I become a special person for Him and only for Him.

Love! Love! All those things love will do unto me, yet I yield so I know the deepest secrets of his heart and in that knowledge become a fraction of his love.

But if I fear love, it will stay away from me. This type of love will leave me, never to return and my days will be long and lonely.

My heart asks: "Shall I pass out of love threshing floor and allow it to walk away and leaving me to a season less days, months, or years, where there will be, no love, no joy, no words of kindness, a world with pure weeping and waiting, all of my tears will drop on the ground like pearls waiting to be scooped up by my very own lover"?

I knew this kind of love. It gave nothing and took nothing but from itself. I yielded but would not be possessed nor allowed me to possess it.

THIS LOVE! OH, THIS LOVE! IT IS SUFFICIENT IN ITS OWN WAY.

TIP:

LOVE IS LOVE IS LOVE IS LOVE; BE OPEN TO RECEIVE.

My Attitude Toward My Exes

I cannot change my ex or seeing them come to take responsibility for their children

But I can change my attitude towards them

I cannot change my past with the pain and the fights and the sleepless nights

But right now, I have made up my mind to have a better future for me and my two boys; I cannot fight all my battles that life throws at me as a single mum

But I can learn to choose those that are worth fighting for.

I cannot get the money and friends that I have lost over the years,

But I will never allow it to face me out

I cannot ever make up for the imperfection in my life

But as from now on I will focus on the positive things in my life and what I have achieved as a single mum

I cannot stop the storms of life hitting my children

But I will teach them to stand stronger and fight a good fight,

I cannot do everything the right way.

But I will equip my children with the tools that they need to survive in this world to make them to become better men.

I cannot do everything that people are expecting me to do or to be a good mum, a daughter, a wife, best friend,

But I can be the best mum that my boys ever needed.

"I can never change someone's attitude but accept them for who they are"

"To love is divine; you are divine"

GOLDEN AGE DATING

"I must not dwell on the past I must concentrate on the future" Golden Age

GOLDEN AGE

Hatred paralyses life, love releases life, Hatred confuses life, love complements it, Hatred darkens life, love illuminates it.

I tried to imagine all the people who were in my life as my own personal emotional trainers since their actions and behaviors toward me, made me tougher, stronger, and more determined to make it in life. It was important for me to speak and act in a positive way no matter what my exes had done. I am a great believer that if I acted in pure love this would help me to bring up my children in a home full of happiness. For the next man who came long, I would not have to wait for him to make me happy as he would only add on to what I had already built by myself and for my children.

REASONS FOR SINGLEDOM

There were numerous reasons why people may be single, for example: coming out of a serious relationship, deciding to take a break from the opposite sex or losing a partner. For me, I decided to take a break from dating after the father of my youngest and I broke up, this allowed me to focus on raising my child, build a business and create a comfortable home. I am glad I made those choices. I also I found out that going on a first date after a long time being alone could be very scary. For example, an occasion where a date had been arranged and he may have eaten before; then there would be no need for him to pay the bill, so I ended up paying. Especially if he sneaked off to the toilet or where we have gone to a wine bar or restaurant that was inappropriate for the type of person I am.

Being out of the dating game for while has left me scared at not knowing what to do, say, act or what to talk about. As a single mother I felt I had passed the 'sell-by date' and would remain on the shelf with nobody giving me a look as they walked by to a 'newer product'. I was scared and worried a new man would not take me seriously and that my body had seen better days, no matter how much I exercised or did diets. My body looking and laughing at   me, saying:

"I'm not going up there again; remember I'm not 21 anymore!"

I was very scared because I felt I was no longer emotionally important enough to change anyone else's life let lone my own. I was very scared in sharing my dreams with a new lover because I felt my dreams would be embarrassing and make him laugh. I was scared I would be exposed to a new way of doing things and not only that – was I ready to learn? There were times I would hold back, too scared to speak my mind or express my feelings. Mainly because I did not want to upset this potential new man in my life and even though I knew what he could end up doing could be wrong for me.

I may have felt all the above, but I still stepped out and took chances. However, before doing so, one must work on self-esteem, confidence, and what we want in a man and what our expectations are from a relationship.

First dates can be scary and can fail, yet they can also be laced with happy endings. Nowadays, I say; be prepared for the unexpected but I also relax, enjoy yourself and the experience.

TIP:

Don't let your past painful experiences stop you from enjoying what life has to offer. Take everything about you with love, happiness, and laughter! Regardless of what ever age you maybe...

"It is scary dating again, just embrace the experience"

Meaningless

Meaningless, meaningless I utter the words slowly, slowly, slowly.

I worked hard, I played hard,

I have had every man my heart desired

I lived my life in the fast lane, society girl that was my name.

My friends called me by that name (Society Girl). That was meaningless I was the soul of the party, always in the spotlight telling jokes, getting drunk, falling flat on my face.

That was cool because everybody loved me. Being seen at the right place with the right People was not life wonderful.

All that was meaningless.

My heart was aching, searching for more, searching for love.

Chasing after the wind, material things, wild life still hoping it would cure my loneliness, gathering things of no importance.

But all that was meaningless in my life without God. My life was meaningless without God.

My life now has a purpose; My life has a destiny,

My life was meaningful because I had God in my life. I am in the spotlight, the spotlight was God.

The spotlight of eternal light of life.

"Negative things previously done mean nothing, it's the positive with the Creator at the helm that means something"

MY BEAUTIFUL PUB LOVER

It was a beautiful summer day! The sun was shining, karaoke music blazing, people singing, kids running around, and beer glasses clinking! Joy was in the air with laughter, dancing, and loud music. I felt good! It was going to be a great day! The tills were busy too.

Two weeks before I had broken up with a long-term lover. He did not want me to open the pub and in the last days we constantly argued. I had moved on with my life and, at the time, deep within, I felt a bit of jealousy coming from him. When I opened the pub, I did not see him until three weeks later and when I asked why, he was absent at the opening day, he told me he was busy. After that, I saw him every few weeks, which turned into months. I called him a few times but his phone went unanswered; so that was the end of our relationship. A very painful breaking up with him since we had been going out for nearly six years and I really needed his support and love. After that experience, I was lonely, burnt out from running the pub, and so went on the rebound.

One day, a gorgeous, handsome man smartly dressed with everything in place walked into the pub. Some of the women, who knew him, greeted him while others were all over him but he paid them no mind. Walking to the bar area, he came directly to me. I asked one of the bar staff to serve him. He smiled and said he wanted me to serve him and would wait for me.

Some of the lads offered to buy him drinks but he declined, saying he could order his own drink. I finished serving other clients and went to him for his order. I was very nervous, but he laughed while talking with the other punters.

Meanwhile the women in the pub were trying to get his attention and they asked him to buy them a drink or offered to buy him one. But he did not entertain them. I wanted to close the pub for lunch when he decided to play the game machine by slotting in large amounts of money. He was not going anywhere and he made me aware by ordering more drinks and telling me if I wanted to close the pub this would be okay. He said I should not worry since everything was going to be all right. Three customers remained and I left a staff member minding the bar, went upstairs to check on my family and rest before opening up for the evening.

He began to come to the pub more often and we would talk a lot. He made me laugh and would help me at closing times even assisting when I was short staffed. He would even bring me little gifts. I started to feel comfortable around him. Then one day he asked me out, I couldn't believe it. I said yes since he was everything I was looking for in a man. He was helpful and good with the children (my youngest was only six months old at the time), he would also buy toys for children.

A few months into the relationship, I began to notice the cracks. He would drink too much and would become nasty to people around him; not to me at first but the bar staff who knew him well. Eventually, one-day one staff member warned me: "Be careful! He can be a live-wire".

He was far too late with the warning since I was already too deep into the relationship with this man and there was no way of escaping it right then.

One day we went for dinner when my phone rang. It was one of my staff members calling me. He suddenly snatched my phone, throwing down and smashing it! Upset I picked up the pieces and left and by the time he came outside, I was already in my car. I drove off.

I returned to the pub ensuring I was not downstairs, instead asking one of my staff members to close up for me. He returned later on, and I told everyone upstairs not to open the door to him but after closing time, he came around and started ringing the doorbell but the door stayed closed. I did not see him again for a few days but I was walking on eggshells, waiting for him to walk in the pub without any warning, at any time. I was scared, not only for myself but for my children. If anything happened to me, what would happen to them? I tried acting normally as much as I could while watching the doors wondering when he would charmingly stroll in like nothing had happened.

One night, three weeks later, I received a call from him asking if he could come to my home. I said, no. This was my only chance to be stronger, but I was a bit scared, knowing he could turn up at any time. Over the days, he would call, and our conversation would go back and forth. He would tell me how much he loved me and wanted to be with me and not to worry, as he would never hurt my family; that worried me even more or me. My fear had hit the roof and was out of control. For another three days, I did not hear from him and the pub was doing really well with the cash intake. There was joy and laughter and my fear subsided, I was no longer on red alert as I had been before. Closing time came and one member of the local football team the pub supported decided to stay behind until we had cashed out the tills and turned off the lights. The player left but before I could retire upstairs, there was a knock on the door. It was my ex. He was back.

Unaware of who it was, I opened the door, laughing and joking, "What have you forgotten now?"

He pushed me aside and closed the door. He asked, "Are you going to offer me a drink?"

I looked at him forcing myself not to be scared, stepped back a safe distance so that he could not reach me but there was nowhere to go, and everyone else was sleeping upstairs. Before I could think of any other action, he jumped over the bar, his hands suddenly around my throat.

"Do you know that I can kill you here and nobody would know I did it? I have not been here for weeks and nobody saw me come in."

I told myself not to answer or show any fear even though my insides were trapped in fear. I do not know how long his hand tightened around my windpipe as he tried to kiss and lick my face. He carried on speaking, and I kept telling myself to standstill and not show any fear. I kept repeating those words. I have no idea what happened next, but his hand dropped away, and he said, "You know what I like about you. You're strange, not scared of anybody – I like that in a woman. "He then jumped over the bar and was gone.

 I locked the pub door and went upstairs crying my eyes out. I then took a long shower. The following morning, I called the brewers and put the pub up for sale. Three weeks later, he returned but I was already packed and ready to move away from the area. I had not told him I was leaving and hoped the people in the pub would not either. It was difficult to act normal since the punters were asking why I was leaving but I told them business was bad and was not doing well, which was true. I put my house up for sale and had to do so because he knew where I lived. He called my phones a few times and I changed the number. I became stressed and soon, I moved away from the area but by then I had a nervous breakdown and was suffering from depression. Living with my sister I refused to leave her home, other than take my son to school and back. That went on for about a year or more before I finally began to be my true self again.

"The signs are always there"

NOTHING TO OFFER

As single mothers, we tend to be written off by society because it feels we have nothing to offer. We have a lot to give because everyone has needs, everyone has a problem, and we may be the ones who could solve those problems.

As single mothers, we may hold the key, which turns the lock that can free other people who face some kind of difficulty.

We speak to other people by uplifting them to leave the road of rejection, loneliness, and depression, yet supporting them on to their road to success.

We can bring a smile or a ray of sunshine in another person's life.

We can be the medicine a person may need at that time by encouraging them in their time of need.

As a single mum our optimism has carried us through some difficult times so we know our optimism can help to support others in overcoming their challenges.

Our friendships can fill the void of loneliness someone feels in their life.

Our faith and belief in others to achieve brings changes needed in their life.

The love we have for our children can bring in a much needed change in other parents lives.

We help others to discover their true self by sharing our journey and experience.

We can answer other personal questions that may not be lone parent related.

The signs are always there. Follow your heart. Listen too hers sometimes. Heed the warnings. Then flee.

"There's always something to learn – or to give"

PHENOMENAL WOMAN

Phenomenal Woman was my second anthem I read when I was going through difficult times. When relationships ended it was time to move to a better life, preparing myself for other broken hearts, broken promises, rejections but within all this I would not dwell on it too long because I already knew the outcome and what I needed to do before we parted company.

Phenomenal Woman – by Maya Angelou

Pretty women wonder where my secret lies.

I'm not cute or built to suit a fashion model's size But when I start to tell them,

They think I'm telling lies. I say,

It's in the reach of my arms, The span of my hips,

The stride of my step, The curl of my lips.

I'm a woman Phenomenally. Phenomenal woman,

 That's me.

I walk into a room

Just as cool as you please, And to a man,

The fellows stand or

Fall down on their knees. Then they swarm around me, A hive of honeybees.

I say,

It's the fire in my eyes, And the flash of my teeth, The swing in my waist, And the joy in my feet.

I'm a woman Phenomenally. Phenomenal woman, That's me.

Men themselves have wondered What they see in me.

They try so much

 But they can't touch My inner mystery.

When I try to show them, They say they still can't see. I say,

It's in the arch of my back, The sun of my smile,

The ride of my breasts, The grace of my style. I'm a woman Phenomenally.

Phenomenal woman, That's me.

Now you understand

Just why my head's not bowed. I don't shout or jump about

Or have to talk really loud. When you see me passing, It ought to make you proud.

I say,

It's in the click of my heels, The bend of my hair,

the palm of my hand, The need for my care. Cause I'm a woman phenomenally.

Phenomenal woman, that is Me.

A Phenomenal Woman!

> *"YOU ARE A PHENOMENAL WOMAN"*

I WOULD LOVE YOU TO STAY

When the morning light appears; and the clatter of footsteps and cars passing by, on the pavement outside his window.

Slowly easing my day into existence, it will be time for me to say goodbye. If only I could stay a bit longer;

I would love to stay dear, to stay, until the sound of coffee cups

comes alive from the kitchen, next door from his bedroom.

The aroma of bacon, eggs, and toast, reeks across the room.

If only I could stay a little bit longer; If only I could stay a little bit longer, But I cannot stay,

because my dear darling this relationship is not working for me.

I want to be loved,

I want to be taken care of,

 I want to feel wanted, not for what you can get from me.

If only I can stay;

If only I can stay,

If only I can stay, my darling. Goodbye! Goodbye my darling! I will shut the front door behind me before he noticed that I left.

If only I could stay.

"Stay"

THE HOTEL ROOM

The lights had been switched out, the laughter stopped,

the reflection of neon lights flashed brightly across the hotel room.

My new lover fast asleep;

I stood across the room looking out the window, my heart beating fast, asking the questions; What are you doing here?

What are you doing here?

Marvin Gay playing, "Let's get it on" in the background. The champagne is finished;

The candle lights stopped flickering; the soft blue light turned into red light.

I looked across the room, my new lover still fast asleep. My heart throbbing asking the same questions as before,

What are you doing here?

What are you doing here?

It's time for you to go,

It's time for you to go.

I gently picked up my clothes and left before dawn catches up with me.

Goodbye! My new lover, Goodbye! My new love.

I cannot stay; you may just turn into a toad rather than a prince, when day light breaks.

> *"It's time to go, sometimes; as hard as it is"*

SHOPPING CHAT-UP LINE

I was rushing around, picking up lunch one afternoon and while in the sandwich area choosing sandwiches and salad for my staff, I felt someone behind me. I turned and saw a lovely man behind me. Apologising, I moved to one side making space for him. I quickly picked what I needed and went to checkout but inside me I felt I was being watched. I looked over my shoulder and it was the same guy. Our eyes met as I reached the cashier and I mentally hurried her since I wanted to get out before he caught me but as I stepped to the doors, he was right there, behind me.

"Excuse me!" He called.

I stopped, putting on my best smile, waiting for him to say something. He handed me a card, went on to say he was a plumber, and did central heating maintenance, "Have you got anything in your house that needs fixing?" He asked. I thought, the look in your eyes tells me you're not marketing or promoting your business.

"No I don't have anything in my house that need fixing," I replied.

He said, "Well, my name and my number are on the card, call me if you do need anything fixing."

I looked at the card and thought, man you need to go to a chat school, if there's a thing like that. Do I look that desperate that I need something fixed? I know I've not been in the dating world for a while but please you can do better than this.

"Call me," he said as he walked away. I stood there for a while watching him and smiled to myself: has the dating world changed so much since the last time I was on the scene? What happened to the cornier chat up lines?

"Haven't I seen you somewhere before?" "Didn't we meet at that night club?"

"Is your name Sue?"

"Can I talk to you for a minute?"

"When are you free for a drink or dinner?"

"I'm free, you can take me out for a drink and you can then have your wicked way with me"

"You have a beautiful smile; can I speak to your brown eyes?"

"Your place or mine?"

"Let me take you out for a night out in the town."

"Let's go and paint the town red then come to my place for a night forgoing and a tick and slap (in a fun) or you are in a night club, he parted the Red Sea of people trying to get to you offering to buy you a drink holding on to you for the whole night dancing and your lips gently brushing one another and yet you both will not dare to kiss."

I got into my car, looked at the card knowing my own personal central heating had not been serviced for nine years and was long overdue for an M.O.T. I knew one thing: you're not going to service this boiler today or any other day. All my pipes are in excellent order until the right man comes along. Putting the card into my car's glove compartment, I drove off.

TIP:

Patience is a virtue.

The 'right' man will appear. He always does. Being in a hurry can cause anxiety and work against you.

Take time to explore.

Have fun and enjoy the journey.

"Lighten up! Have fun and enjoy!"

GO AWAY, I'M MARRIED!

It was a beautiful sunny Saturday, and I awoke on my own again like so many, many Saturdays before but this time this one was different. I had a good rest. Slept well and awoke with joy in my heart! I was going to meet my friends for a drink and catch up. I had not been out for a while as I had been busy being a single mother and businesswoman. It was not easy trying to date at the same time, with the school runs, school holidays, last minute dot com school trips; I could not juggle all the balls so I dropped one - the dating ball.

I was asked on a date by this great looking gentle speaking guy and took my time in getting dressed. Later we met at a venue since I did not allow him to come and collect me from my home; not like back in the old days when I would have allowed it. I told him to give me the address and I would meet him there. We met at a restaurant but had twenty minutes before it closed. Still, we sat to eat and that was when he told me he had already eaten.

"You can go and get food from the buffet", he said. When I got there, the food was almost gone and even when I took some food, my plate was still almost empty.

He asked, "Aren't you hungry?"

I looked at him trying to compose myself. I was starving and by this time dreading the rest of the evening. We went to a pub he frequently used and he asked what I wanted to drink. I told him: orange juice, and went looking for our seats. He brought our drinks over, sat and said, "I don't like drinking outside, I prefer drinking inside, at home."

I quickly drank and said it was time for me to go. I thought, goodbye my friend, you were not for me.

My youngest was away for the weekend and I did not have to worry about him since he was with my brother and his cousins. I had the house to myself and the only person I needed to worry about was me. Taking a shower, I chose a long flowing summer dress that complemented my figure. I had breakfast, which I did not do often since I was always too busy. After thoroughly enjoying it, I realised I did not have to worry about my son as he was not around. I went upstairs and re-brushed my teeth, applied bright red lipstick (when I was younger I felt wearing bright red lipstick would make my dark complexion shine like the early morning sunrise!) and I felt good and confident as I left the house.

I got into my car, put on my cool shades, and checked in the mirror making sure everything was in place, then drove off to a nearby shopping Centre; there I took my time strolling and window-shopped. As I stood outside a jeweler's shop a man reflection smiled at me and said, "You look good."

I did not answer him as I was not in the mood for small chat or to be chatted up, I just wanted to enjoy my day. The next thing I knew, there were footsteps, and he was beside me.

"You look nice," he said again. "Thank you," I replied.

I wanted to cut the conversation short as I did not want to be bothered and I was searching for a bracelet (it had been a long time since I treated myself since any spare cash I did have, seemed to always be spent on unexpected bills). I went inside without giving him a second chance to say anything more and hoped that by the time I left the shop he would have received the message that I was not interested. I took my time looking around the shop but did not see anything I really liked but every time I looked up, he was standing there watching me. In the end I bought a bracelet I had not budgeted for and every time I stared through the window; he was there staring at me. In the end, I told myself, I needed to go and of course, he was still outside.

As I came out of the shop, he shouted, "Are you married"?

I stopped, turned and shouted back, "Yes I am married to Jesus! Now piss-off! Go away and stop harassing me!!"

When I returned to my car, I was being really hard on myself - why did I tell that man I was married? I could have asked him to come into the jeweler's with me and buy the bracelet. Why had I allowed him to spoil my beautiful day? I could have been in control of myself a bit more but at least my friends were going to have a good laugh when I told them about it!

TIP

It's ok, just don't be too hard on yourself. Just remember not everybody is a 'threat' or wishing to date you –immediately.

They my just wish to be courteous and polite.

"It's ok to be hard on yourself, just don't do it too often!!"

PLAYING WITH MY FEELINGS

You just cannot keep playing with my feelings because you think you can,

You cannot keep playing with my emotions because you feel you can.

This is what I have to say to you:

If you cannot be a grown Man walk on by, If you cannot see me for who I am.

Please, Please, just walk on by because there is no room for jerks,

If you cannot accept me because I am a powerful and successful businesswoman,

Do not stand round just walk on by.

If you are threatened by my success and by my popularity, Baby, baby just walk on by.

If you cannot love the way I want to be loved, Hey just walk on by.

For I am a woman, a successful one, so I do not need you, to come and pay my bills I have done that on my own.

Therefore, so, man just walk on by.

I need a man in my life who wants to be with me not to take me for a fool or for a ride, because you feel you can.

No, no, I am no longer wearing that t-shirt that says I am easily ridden,

If you are not that kind of a man, baby walk on by

Do not leave your coat behind because there is no room in this inn for you.

If you are a man looking for the right woman, I may have a readymade family, but I am willing to open the door to my heart and invite you in,

If you are still willing to come; I will open the door of my heart and let you in.

> *"Feelings are emotions; emotions are energy. Keep the energy that builds and release those that don't!"*

"Feel what you feel and make no apologies"

READY TO DATE

"I must make every day as productive as I can so that I can achieve my dreams"

THE KEY FOR ME FINDING LOVE

I now see life as it is and am grateful for everything I have received, including the struggles I have gone through over the years and what I had learnt from them as I enter golden age. By being grateful and practicing it, many doors have been opened which were once closed. In addition, anything that happened to me throughout any one day I would be thankful for since no matter what it was, I no longer wished to live in a past filled with tears or worry. I also feel a deep gratitude to everyone for being kind to me, enabling me to know the power in changing my negative thoughts, which were holding me captive all my adult life. Now negativity would fall away making room for the positive and wonderful things moving in my life. The more grateful I was, the more I felt good within myself and in getting closer to finding Mr. Right.

As a single mother, my focus was to bring up my children and this responsibility. On top of that, battling the fear of whether my children would be okay and the kind of future they would have since they grew up in a single parent home. I am no longer worrying too much about that because I cannot control their future or destiny but what I need to do now is get to know me.

Who am I? Because of the long single mother journey, I was lost along the way, but I no longer want to carry any baggage into my new life. I made certain I was going to get rid of: *broken promises from past relationships; rejection from family and previous partners; broken heart; hatred;*

Gossiping with my friends about my man, getting the wrong advice; criticizing my partner for anything he was not doing or the way I would like but enabling him to do it his way and as long as he was happy, getting the same result we, both were looking for;

I was going to allow him to be the man he should be in our relationship;

trust him that he would do the right things in both of our lives;

Allowing him to love my family; and me

Allowing him to be part of the decision making because as a single mother I tend to make all the decisions, good or bad;

For me to be helpful and have a supportive partner;

Above all else, for me to love him for him with all his weaknesses and strengths.

> *"Love hurt sometimes but no matter what, do not give up love; for surely it'll come knocking on your door, unexpectedly"*

THE KEY POINTS WHICH WILL HELP YOU

I knew all change began with me since I am looking for a loving relationship. I cannot do the same things I did when I was younger or in my young adult days otherwise, I would keep getting the same results. I have learnt that whatever I gave to others I must give to myself and stop putting myself last. I knew in any relationship I was in, whether a partnership, friends, family, and children; were great channels of learning on how to give and receive love. I would open other doors to change my entire life just to give and receive. In my new relationship, I would give and allow love to be returned, encouraging kindness, and support and have heart-filled gratitude for my new partner.

As I Maneuvered the dating minefield, these were the key points I learnt:

To look for things I loved to see in a relationship, staying away from the negatives or a wishing to see the relationship come to an end and make every effort in ensuring it worked.

To stick at it, looking at how I needed the relationship to work for the both of us.

To focus on the excellent qualities he would bring and looked to him as my emotional and personal trainer.

Not criticise, blame, complain, nag or find fault with him and would support him so that we could have a better relationship.

Try not to change him or know what was best for him, asking him what he expected from us - our relationship - so that we could have a happier and a lasting one.

To change the way I looked at things, by not comparing myself to others and their relationships.

Stop running around trying to change bad situations within my relationship by seeking and accepting advice from friends or other people who were unqualified to do so.

To feel positive about myself and know who I am, the right man would see it.

TO LEARN TO LOVE ME.

The more love I give out there, the more love would return to me.

Importantly, I must always remember there is such a thing as a small act of kindness and every act of kindness will create a great ripple of positivity in my life and my children's lives.

THE KEY OF DISCOVERING ME

As a single mother I forgot about myself and my own happiness since all of my attention was focused on being a good mother, father, and provider. It was not easy, but I have done it, my two boys are grown, doing their own things. Over the years the fun went out the window but now I am ready to discover how to have fun in dating, laughing a lot more and enjoying life again as a free single woman. I looked at the opportunities in my life where it was not the right time either because I was too busy to receive them, financial restrictions or just scared. So now I am re-learning to have fun, going out and doing things I was unable to do.

I used the law of attraction and knew I had everything I needed like joy and happiness, good relationships and good health to do all the things I wanted to do but could not because of my children. I learnt that every spare moment was an opportunity waiting for me and now that I am out there dating, I am sure I would meet Mr. Right and not Mr. Make-Do like I used to think and accept. I told myself I was not good enough to I have a good man in my life but as from today I have changed my mind set and would not settle for anything less anymore in my life. So goodbye Mr. Make-Do and welcome Mr. Right.

TIP:

Be who you are, love who you are, be happy who you are, and love will find you-that's Law of Attraction.

"I love Law of Attraction; it works every time!"

MY NEW FOUND LOVER

Dearest New Lover when you are tired let me be the one you come to rest on,

When you are in darkness let my smile light up your path.

When you tire of carrying the entire family's load, allow me to come and help make it lighter for you.

When you are fearful and defenseless, please let me come and put my arms around you, chasing that fear away.

When you feel lonely, let me be the one to come and comfort you.

When you are weary and helpless let me be the one to come, comfort and motivate you.

I will be all those things to you because I love you.

> *"Let me help you light the way, my new found love!"*

I Come as a Package

I come as a package so any man who would like to date me should know I have a different set of rules especially since I factor my children into any decision I make. So, dating as a single mother would always take a backseat to the needs of my children. As a single parent, I came to my role because both of my previous partners left me; others become single parents for various reasons.

I have learnt to be independent and stronger in facing life's storms. I have learnt how to run my household and it was tough at the time but when my youngest child was about fourteen,

I felt ready to return to the dating game and now I no longer think about the father, no longer obsessed about him not being around to help.

There were times when I needed grown-up conversation and someone to be there for me but that was like climbing Mount Everest or needing a compass to find my way through the dudes and dorks when seeking that nice and caring man.

TIP:

A package comes in all shapes and sizes and as a single parent; no decision should be made without considering them.

WHERE WOULD I FIND MR. RIGHT AT MY AGE?

Now that I am ready to meet Mr. Right, how do I find him? We could have met at a school PTA meeting but that never happened since they were either married or had a partner and those who were single looked like they did not want a relationship at all because their hands were full with the ups and downs of being a lone parent. Where else? In the supermarket, on the sideline at my child's football game or in a bookstore. I looked there too but nobody who I would want to bring home and introduce to my two boys ever presented himself. I did have a few who approached me in the supermarket. Others I approached by asking for help, like reaching for a box of cereal on the top shelf and if I liked them, would strike up a conversation with a view of it going further. Sometimes though, he would just say a few things and I would be off running. In our Golden Age, where do we go and meet Mr Right. Clubbing is out of the question for me. So where do all Golden Agers go? Because dating is not what we once knew, for new techniques have taken over.

TIP:

Finding in somebody is easy, it's whether you're ready to so or not.

SINGLE MOTHER'S FACE UNIQUE CHALLENGES

As a single parent, I sometimes gave so much to others that I end up living in deficit - physically, emotionally, and spiritually- drained.

To stay healthy, I refreshed myself and try to be in a good frame of mind every day. I needed to be positive and prayed a lot for God's help, especially the times I could not put food on the table or pay my bills. The word "single parent" I somewhat found to be contradiction.

TIP:

Being a single mother is a wonderful blessing. Enjoy it.

SEARCHING FOR LOVE

To the father of my children, I had given up in search of your love,

For years, I had been with you, losing sight of who I was and what made me happy.

Instead of sitting around, waiting for you to come and take your responsibilities, I chose to go it alone.

No longer with regrets, I would take a chance in love again. My new love, my new love;

It may be scary for you to have my children and me in your heart but guess what; it was just as scary for me.

From your view point it was not just one person's heart to look after, but two or three broken hearts in need of repair.

Taking in bruised and battered emotions in need of love and healing.

Taking on my stubborn self and cute innocent children who did not know they needed you as yet,

One day you will become their step- father and that will be a lot for you to take in.

I knew you would play a huge role which might be scary but would be worth it, when you feel valued and loved and needed every day in our lives.

Your time spent with us would not be wasted since you were much loved and appreciated.

I would try my hardest to be what you deserved, what you needed me to be.

I am not here to break your heart or play games; I am here to love you as you will love my children and me.

I would hold nothing back from you but give you all I have to give.

I chose to wake up every day reminding myself I was strong, beautiful, kind, loving, honest, hardworking, funny and worthy of being loved; the way I want to be loved. One day I would get that kind of love from a man who would take my hand, walk with me down the aisle and say - I do - in front of my friends, family and children.

"Seek and you shall find, love is one of those things, it's just about being open when it does find you"

FINDING THE RIGHT ONE

Dear reader,

You're beautiful, amazing, and worthy of so much love. Don't you ever forget that.

I woke up with the feeling of finding; someone special,

that will love me for who I am. I walked the crowded streets; in the hope to find,

the man of my dreams,

to meet and he will whisper,

the sweet four letter word L.O.V.E. I am in this world for a purpose; to be loved and love back,

to have friends, around me, yet, I am still alone.

I stand on these crowded streets; lovers walking by, holding hands. Whispering the sweet words,

that I long to hear, 'I LOVE YOU'.

But, for how long? My unfulfilled heart,

silently I have to wait for love to start.

"How, how long do I have to wait for you my LOVE"?

"Make it last forever"

I Would Love You to Stay

As a single mother and dating it tended to be very
difficult since some men thought of you as being
desperate and unable to do without them! Some think
they were the best thing that could have ever
happened to you while some would like to treat you
as their personal booty call - if you allowed them.
Others do not stay long enough to know you or your
children and as a lone parent you know you cannot
afford to go down the booty call road because of your
child/children since you do not want them seeing too
many men coming and going from your home and
bedroom like a revolving door. All you think of is to
protect your children and ensure no man came and
abused them. So, in the end, you stayed on your own.

After my son's father walked away for the second
time, I focused on rearing my son and starting a new
business. My son was nine years old at the time (he is
now 18). I was very lonely. I wanted to go on dates
but was fearful as I did not want any man to abuse my
son or took advantage of me because they felt I
needed them more than they needed me.
Furthermore, I did not want to pick any man who
wanted to be a kept man - sitting on my settee, taking
over the TV or me paying all the bills. So, I decided
that in the end, it was not worth the hassle. Now, my
son was eighteen years of age, doing his own thing,
ready to go on a date since I no longer worry about
him, both boys would ask me when I go on a date:

175

"When are you coming home?" "Who are you going with?"

"Make sure they bring you home on time."

Somehow how our roles have reversed.

I recently went on a date and found it very difficult. It seemed the rules of the dating game had changed. On our first outing, he spoke so well of the kind of person he was and that for a long time had not been with any woman since he was waiting for the right one. He said he was looking for a long-lasting relationship and that sounded so good. One day he invited me to visit where lived outside of London. At first, I did not want to go until one day I submitted. I must say he was good since he cooked and made me feel really relaxed. Then he said he would like to go shopping, taking me to a camping shop since he was going camping soon. When we got there he asked me to buy a tent. I was shocked. I could hardly believe it; this man was asking me to buy his tent. I honestly thought he must have been joking as I looked at him: "What are you saying? Are you kidding me?"

He looked at me and asked: "Are you going to buy it for me?"

I was so appalled by his behaviour and as much as I wanted to be with him, at the back of my mind I kept thinking he was mean and after three months of dating, I walked away. Saying to myself that if I waited this long for Mr. Right, I was not about to allow any man treat me like 'Miss Money Bags'.

I have finally grown tired of kissing frogs, hoping against hope that one day one of them would turn into my Prince Charming and as of that day I refused to kiss any more frogs

> ## TIP:
>
> *Sometimes it takes a while to find the 'right' one but there's no need to be desperate.*

"It's a marathon, not a sprint or a gallop!"

MY FUTURE LOVE

As a single lone parent;

I will not fall for you all at one go, no, I will not do that,

I will fall for you gradually, slowly, and easy bring me, to the point I know who you are.

I am falling in love with you; as I stood aside watching you,

as you play fun games with my children,

I am falling in love with you gradually, as my children will come to you for help,

I will fall in love with you,

as I see you do silly little things, that will make my children and I, laugh with joy in our hearts.

I will gradually, very gradually;

fall in love with you as we steal few moments, to ourselves without the children noticing us. I will, I will fall in love with you;

as we go for food shopping, and the children start to play up, and how you gently correct them,

and hold their little hands, cross the road with them. I will, I will, gradually fall in love with you;

when we go out on a family outing,

and you will do silly things like chase us round the park, pushing my young son on the swing hearing him laugh, with happiness in his heart.

I will love you, love you;

as you stood in the kitchen cooking dinner, for your new ready-made family.

I will love you, love you;

when you see me for who I am,

and not intimated by the way I look in the morning, as I get the children ready for the school run,

and how you will come and join me and help.

I will love you, love you gradually but not all at once; as you take time out from work and send me a text,

that will make me laugh and brighten the rest of my day.

I will love you, love you; oh, how I will love – gradually,

 as you reach over to me still sleeping,

in your fogged state and pull me close to you, as if you cannot keep me close enough.

I will love you, love you;

as we laugh together seeing how truly, you love me and how your eyes, will search the core deeper in me,

that will reveal all my flaws, and my vulnerability, to you and you will wisp gently,

in my heart and tell me how much you need me, and my children in your life.

I will never break your heart;

because you are the most beautiful thing, that has ever happened to me.

I will, I will; oh, I will fall in love with you and will shout it out from the roof tops,

and hold you close to my heart never, never letting you go.

"Nobody knows what tomorrow brings, we might as well allow love to find us"

POEMS OF LIFE

"Attitude is a little thing that makes a big difference"

THE COLOUR OF YOUR SKIN

This poem is dedicated to all the women who have lost their sons through knife crime. Stephen Lawrence life was cut short because of the Colour of his skin; a young man full of promise, his light shining brightly while he was here on earth. Born into the right family, they exposed the deeply embedded racism within the police and fought hard to bring about changes in the way they operated. They also ensured the newspaper's kept the story on their front pages and thus in people's hearts and minds.

When I wrote this poem my older son was only four years old and I was so worried that something like Stephen's death could happen to him. Thank goodness my son has grown up well and is safe.

The Poem: The Colour Of Your Skin

What a beautiful life; Cut short because of the Colour of your skin.

My son! My son! My son!

Did I tell you how much I love you? I love you! I love you! I love you!

My son! My son!

 Did I teach you all the things?

that a mother should teach her son?

All the right things you need to know about life? Stand up strong!

Hold your head up high! Fight for your beliefs!

Always do your best in everything you do. Work hard at school;

get a good education, get a career,

care for yourself, love yourself, respect yourself, above all be you. My son! My son!

Have I told you lately, that I love you? I love you! I love you! I love you!

My son! My son!

Did I teach you to be honest? "a law-abiding citizen"?

 To care for your fellow human beings?

That everybody is the same regardless of the colour of their skin, their sex or their religion?

Love them and accept them, for whom they are.

Oh! My son!

Even though life can be so cruel and hard you feel that you can no longer go on!

Lift your head high and smile,

Say, "I am in charge of my life and my destiny No one can take that away, because I am a child of the Most High God". My son! My son! My son!

Have I told you lately, that I love you? I love you! I love you! I love you!

My son! My son! My son!

I know I taught you

all that a mother needs to teach a son Though you have gone from this earth, you are still the light in my heart, burning brightly,

a light no man can take away from me. My son! My son! My son!

I am proud of you, I am proud of you,

I was proud of you when you were alive.

I am even more proud of you now that you are gone.

You are my hero.

My heart! My life! My soul! I love you, my son.

Even though your life was cut short, You have touched millions of lives and millions of people

have learnt from your death. My son! My son!

There is a big hole in my heart,

There is an even bigger hole in the world,

because they have missed out what you came to teach them. My son! My son! My son!

I love you! I love you! I love you!

'I pay homage to you'.

"Honour those who honour you"

ALL THE PERFORMANCES IN MY LIFE

When I was younger, I felt we were all here to perform.

All of us on a stage; the stage of life. From the minute we were born, we were on the stage; it would then be up to us on how we performed. Some of us acted excellently, some okay, some not so good, some very badly and still others blamed other people for how they acted, some exited early as soon as they became tired of life and like actors, performed differently to their own changing script and drama.

The first people on this stage were our parents. From when we were born, they set and wrote our first script, our first drama. They were the directors, our cheerleaders, the audience. They could also write our downfall. But the time would come when our parents leave our stage, leaving us alone to write for ourselves and how we write that script would depend on us.

Onto this stage other performers have also entered - siblings, friends, husbands, children and even lovers; bosses, pastors; unexpected events and new businesses carry significant changes and shape into our lives. Many would leave during and in the middle of the performance; a permanent emptiness. And when we realised their part on our stage had come to an end, we must let them go.

Many actors would leave unnoticed, vacating without your knowledge, thank them since they too added a little bit of colour into your life.

The stage could be filled with joy, sorrow, fantasy, expectations, hellos, goodbyes, and happiness but we would still need to perform to the best of our ability, as the show must go on with no getting off to say goodbye or pulling the final curtain. No matter how tough it would get, you must keep on going since better days are always ahead. Moreover, sometimes an excellent performance comes by having someone helping you, loving you for who you were and not whom he or she think you should be. On this stage, giving your best performance through the hard and difficult times or even painful moments was all you could give even though the script sometimes changed.

In the end, we do not know when we will leave this world and when we will have our final performance but until then we live the best way we can, adjusting the script from time to time, never forgetting to forgive or to offer the best of what we have to our co-performers. We should leave behind beautiful memories for those who would continue performing on this stage called life.

"I thank you, all of you that may come on my stage of life and perform with me! God Bless all of you for being there for me!"

TIP:

Remember all life is a stage, so is yours; understand the script, embrace the actors, listen to the director. It's for your own good.

189

A VIRTUOUS WOMAN

A Virtuous woman she is clothed:

with strength, dignity, graciousness, compassion, and love. She speaks with wisdom and faithfulness in her heart.

A Virtuous woman, she is the heartbeat of her household; she takes care of the affairs of her house.

Her house would never be in darkness,

nor does she sit and eat from the plate of a deceitful woman,

nor does she transgress.

A virtuous woman, she is more precious than rubies and pearls.

She is the diamond in her husband's eye; Shining brightly like a star.

Her beauty and charms are like an essence of white lily. A virtuous woman holds the world;

She opens out her arms to the poor and extends to the needy.

She is the light of the universe. Her children are called blessed.

They are as fine wine equipped with all the fullness of life; her children would lack nothing,

Her husband stands with righteous men, He would praise his wife.

A virtuous woman has the fear of the Lord Jesus Christ;

Because she knows that, she is clothed with the love of Jesus.

Her work would never go unnoticed.

By Margaret Thorli

"I am the best there is, there will never be another!"

"Dance like nobody is watching, scream as if you want the world to hear and move because you want the world to see"

MY SINGLE MOM CV

A single mother you need to be good at almost everything, if not, you need to be prepared to learn very quickly or look to spend a lot of money on call out fees. Therefore, for me I had no choice but do so quickly as I went on, or things would become stressful and frustrating.

Personal Profile: hard working, fun to be with, caring, very patient, kind, ready to listen to both sides of a problem, ready and prepared for emergencies, fearless and ready for battle in short notice, defend their children, heart as hard as a walnut, hard from the outside but sweet when protecting her children.

Key skills

Emergency Officer

Chief Financial Officer

Data Management Specialist Staff Mediator

Household Representative, Project Manager,

Private Investigator

General Assistant

Executive Officer

Chief Executive House Planer Officer Product Development Expert

Chief Restorer

Financial Analyst

Proprietor

Executive Maintenance Manager Presiding Domestic Office

Chief Time Management Chief Negotiator

Kick Ass Father/Mum

Resources Needed: Goldfish, crackers and Band-Aids are never far away, always ready to raise finance for school trips. Hand sanitizer, chap stick, a small dinosaur, some crayons, reading books, colouring books, quick food, flash- light, and flushable wipes.

Time Management: be excellent in time management, chief administrator, setting day-to-day goals, be patient, always ready to go on a short notice, be a master planner for the next day

Chief Negotiator/Team Builder: You must be ready to negotiate and settle disputes very quickly and ready to build lost relationships. Organise playtime, bedtime clashes and agreements

Chief Financial Officer: Organising all the monthly bills and making sure money stretches for food, shopping, school emergency money and maybe even have extra to spend on non-necessities for the children.

School Runs: Know the many hours of sleep are needed to feel okay for the school runs the next day and picking from after school and be ready for Saturday drama activities.

Interested in something: Whether it is how to live a happier life, maintain better relationships, reading, movies, friends, and partnerships.

The Highest Paid Job: Being a full-time single mum is one of the highest jobs even though it may be stressful and lonely at times. But all the payments come from the purest hearts of our children and that, in itself, is priceless.

Choose Wisely

Do not stand there thinking how you are going to play me with the next woman.

Do not stand there thinking I am a pushover.

You cannot play with my feelings because you are unsure about your own; I will never allow you just because you are a man.

You cannot come and play with my feelings and leave because you feel I am not worth the time or day for you to get to know me.

So, my dear, dearest friend I am choosing wisely, as you are not for me or for my children, walk on by and never look back because I am out of your reach!

Pain is all but temporary; the journey will always be good; depending on your point of view"

ABOUT THE AUTHOR

Margaret Thorli is the founder and director of Hope and Restoration Ltd., trading as H&R Training Professionals. She is an entrepreneur, business coach, mentor, trainer, and international speaker. Margaret has a passion to show people how to massively improve their life with little effort!

In addition to speaking at conferences and organising charity events, Margaret empowers individuals in their personal life and career and shows them how to build their businesses. She has learnt her trade by being positive, proactive and by implementing her plans; she has simply been there and done it, printed the T-shirt and worn the T- shirt.

Her passion for business enterprise started at the young age of 21 when she ventured out as a market trader selling European cosmetics in Islington Market. While in the market, she spotted a gap in Afro-Caribbean cosmetics and therefore went to the USA in search of these cosmetics. Although she found and bought some cosmetics to trade in, when she got back from the U.S. she felt the need to convince some manufacturers and distributors in the UK about the big gap in the market for Afro-Caribbean cosmetic lines. This quest led to the production of a new line of cosmetic products of different colour shades that suited women of colour very well. Her customer base was boosted to such an extent that she set up other market stalls around London and employed people to run them.

After 14 years in the market, she moved into the pub business and became one of the few black women to open and run a pub in Islington. In 2001, she opened a designer clothing and handbag shop in Tottenham, and by 2003 she decided it was time to go back to college and gain some qualifications while at the same time bringing up her two children. In 2004 she secured a job as a school mentor working with children that were about to be excluded from school. From there she began working with young adults and lone parents who were setting up their own businesses.

Margaret was very keen to become successful in her new role as a mentor. She now spends her time training, teaching and mentoring others so that they can achieve their own dreams of running their own businesses or securing the jobs of their dreams. Margaret focuses on what she believes to be the crucial ways anyone can achieve success in business or career. She therefore gives coaching on mindset and belief, letting go of fear, effective ways of goal setting, and challenges her clients to dare to dream.

Margaret is a trainer, a mentor and business coach, encouraging people to succeed in their lives. Margaret is teaching style is very relaxed and she aims to make everything very easy to understand and implement. She achieves this by teaching individuals to use the very tools and techniques that she uses in her everyday life. Furthermore, Margaret speaks internationally at many types of business and leadership events.

NEW ONLINE DATING WORKSHOP

Out Now!!!!

Book Your Space!

Are you tired of the hit and miss dating online?

Ladies you don't have to kiss many frogs to find your prince.

Stop wasting your time kissing frogs it is time for you to kiss your prince.

The single mother and the dating game has a new exciting

Workshop coming up.

This will help you feel confident, comfortable and in control to find your prince charming online.

Contact us to book your place on click the link below and claim a Free Gift!

www.letschangeyourlifewithmargaretthorli.com

mailto:info@margaretthorli.com

http://www.margaretthorli.com

Learn from experiences and dating mistakes

Practical guidance and exercises for you to use

Read proven case studies and stories about the dating minefield

I look forward to working with you

God Bless You Richly

For Your Support!

About The Author

Insert image (don't use copy and paste)

AUTHOR NAME is Margaret Thorli

Find out more at

https://www.amazon.com/author/margaretthorli

Or
visit:www.letschangeyourlifewithmargaretthorli.com

Other Books By (Author)

List your other kindle books with a link to the page

You will need to update your books with this information as you create more books over time

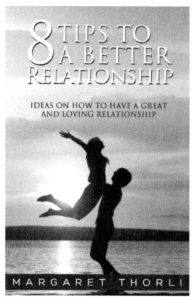

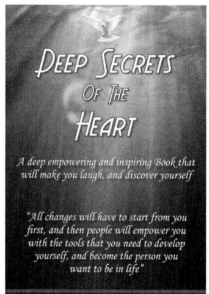

Workbook

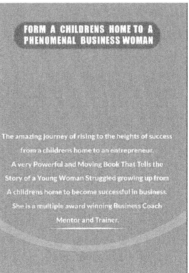

CAN I ASK A FAVOUR?

If you enjoyed this book, found it useful or otherwise then I'd really appreciate it if you would post a short review on Amazon . I do read all the reviews personally so that I can continually write what people are wanting. If you able to please email me copy of review of Testimonials that I can share with my community and websites if you willing to be published let us know if you want your name or just initials on there .

If you'd like to leave a review, then please visit the link below:

Thanks for your support!

https://www.amazon.com/author/margaretthorli

www.letschangeyourlifewithmargaretthorli.com

mailto:info@margaretthorli.com

http://www.margaretthorli.com

Printed in Great Britain
by Amazon

15342628R10120